William Shakespeare

Power and Ambition in Shakespeare

Adaptation and activities by **Jane Cammack**

Illustrated by **Anna and Elena Balbusso**

Editor: Daniela Difrancesco
Design and Art Direction: Nadia Maestri
Computer graphics: Simona Corniola
Picture research: Laura Lagomarsino

© 2012   Black Cat

First edition: January 2012

Picture credits:
t: top, b: bottom, l: left, r: right, c: centre
Photos.com; iStockphoto; Dreamstime ; MAYFAIR
ENTERTAINMENT INTERNATIONAL / Album / CONTRASTO:
17l; JAM - Album / Album / CONTRASTO: 17r; De Agostini Picture
Library: 24, 28, 29, 30, 69, 70, 71, 91; © Robbie Jack/Corbis: 27;
RENAISSANCE FILMS-BBC-CURZON FILM/ Album /
CONTRASTO: 50l; WebPhoto: 50r; M.G.M - Album / Album /
CONTRASTO: 60; CASTLE ROCK ENTERTAINMENT - KONO /
Album / CONTRASTO: 90; © The Print Collector/Corbis: 91;
© Bettmann/CORBIS: 91; Getty Images: 91.

We would be happy to receive your comments and suggestions, and
give you any other information concerning our material.
info@blackcat-cideb.com
blackcat-cideb.com

The Publisher is certified by

C CISQCERT

in compliance with the UNI EN ISO 9001:2008
standards for the activities of «Design and
production of educational materials»
(certificate no. 02.565)

ISBN 978-88-530-1210-4   Book + CD

Printed in Italy by Litoprint, Genoa

Contents

Part two from *Richard III* and Part one from *Hamlet* are downloadable from our website:
www.blackcat-cideb.com.

 These symbols indicate the beginning and end of the passages
 linked to the listening activities.

(@) www.blackcat-cideb.com passage downloadable from our site.

William Shakespeare (1564-1616)

William Shakespeare lived for just fifty-two years. Between 1590 and 1613 he wrote 37 plays, 154 sonnets and a few long poems.

Holy Trinity church in the town of Stratford-upon-Avon, in the central part of England, does not record Shakespeare's birth date, but we know that his baptism took place on 26 April 1564. Baptisms were usually three days after the birth of a child, so William was probably born on 23 April, St. George's Day, the day of England's patron saint.

His father was John Shakespeare, who made fine leather gloves and purses. John was quite a wealthy man when he married Mary Arden, and they had eight children. William, their third child, was born in a house in Henley Street. He attended the Grammar School in Stratford, where he studied Latin, religion, a little mathematics and some Greek. William had to leave school at the age of 13, when his father got into debt. Nothing is known of William's life for the next four years, and the next event that we know about is his marriage.

On 28 November 1582, William married Anne Hathaway. He was 18 and she was 26 and pregnant with their first child, Susanna. Anne moved into the house in Henley Street and two years later twins, Judith and Hamnet, were born. We do not know what Shakespeare did or where he lived from 1582 to 1591, but we do know that in 1592 he was living in London earning his living by acting and writing plays. In 1594 William joined Richard Burbage's acting company, The Lord Chamberlain's Men. Theatre companies needed patrons – rich, important people who gave the companies money to put on plays – and the Lord Chamberlain was an important person at court. William became their most important playwright for the next two decades. Later, in 1603, when James I was on the throne, they changed their name to the King's Men.

The London theatres had to close between 1592 and 1594 because of the spread of the plague – over 33,000 people died in London – and this is when William started writing sonnets. He needed financial aid and the Earl of Southampton became his patron: the sonnets are dedicated to him. William registered his poems because poets were considered serious artists, but he did not publish his plays, as plays were not considered works of art. They were only published seven years after his death in a collection, which is now called 'the First Folio'.

In 1599 Shakespeare's company opened The Globe Theatre, on the south bank of the Thames near Southwark, where most of his plays were performed. The theatre had a globe as its symbol with the motto in Latin: *Totus Mundus Agit Histrionem*, which can be translated more or less as 'All the world is a stage'. The play which they put on to open The Globe was *Henry V*. It was a popular play because it is about the English king Henry V's victories over the French and is full of patriotic feeling.

Between 1590 and 1596 Shakespeare mainly wrote historical plays. His ten comedies were written between 1593 and 1600 and he wrote tragedies between 1595 and 1605. During his twenty-five year stay in London we know that he returned to Stratford in 1596, when his son Hamnet died.

In 1597 William bought New Place, the second largest house in Stratford. He bought land in 1602 and lived in New Place when, in 1610, he retired from his life in the theatre at the age of only 46. He died of a fever at the age of 52 on 23 April 1616.

Shakespeare's Globe Theatre burnt down in 1614, but in 1996 – nearly 400 years after it was first built – a reconstruction was built very near where the original was. Now audiences sit and stand to watch performances there just as they did in the time of Shakespeare.

William Shakespeare's legacy lives on not only through his plays and sonnets but also in the language we use today. Over a thousand words in the English language are recorded for the first time in his plays, and many phrases from the plays have become common expressions: 'break the ice', 'there is method in his madness', and 'the naked truth' are just some examples. Moreover, his plays, characters and themes have inspired operas such as the Italian composer Verdi's *Macbeth* (1847), *Otello* (1887) and *Falstaff* (1893), and music such as Felix Mendelssohn's overture and incidental music for *A Midsummer Night's Dream* (1826). More than 350 films have been made of his plays, and several other films have been inspired by the plots of the plays.

1 **Comprehension check**
Answer the following questions.

1   How have historians calculated Shakespeare's date of birth?
2   Why was Richard Burbage's acting company called The Lord Chamberlain's Men?
3   What was the effect of the plague on London and on Shakespeare?
4   What is the First Folio?
5   In which way did Shakespeare contribute to the English language?

RICHARD III

Before you read

1 Look at the list of characters in the story before you start reading.

Richard: Duke of Gloucester

Buckingham: Richard's right-hand man

King Edward IV: the older brother of Richard and Clarence

Queen Elizabeth: wife of King Edward IV

Clarence: Richard's older brother

Lady Anne: widow of Prince Edward (son of former king, Henry VI), then Richard's wife

Duchess of York: Richard's mother

Margaret: widow of King Henry VI

The princes: the two young sons of King Edward IV

Young Elizabeth: Queen Elizabeth's daughter

Richmond: a member of a branch of the Lancaster royal family

Hastings: a lord who is loyal to the family of Edward IV

Setting: England in around 1485.

2 **Listening**

Listen to the beginning of Part One. We meet Richard at the beginning of the play and discover how evil he is. Decide if each sentence is correct or incorrect. If it is correct put a tick (✓) in the box under A for YES. If it is not correct, put a tick (✓) in the box under B for NO.

		A	B
1	There has been civil war in England.	☐	☐
2	Richard's younger brother is King of England.	☐	☐
3	Richard plans to murder King Edward.	☐	☐
4	King Edward is very ill.	☐	☐
5	Lady Anne is in love with Richard.	☐	☐
6	Richard killed Lady Anne's husband.	☐	☐
7	King Edward and Queen Elizabeth have two young sons.	☐	☐
8	Richard is a friend of Queen Elizabeth.	☐	☐
9	The old Queen Margaret tells Elizabeth that her sons will be kings.	☐	☐
10	Richard has many true friends.	☐	☐

3 **Reading pictures**

Look at the pictures on page 13 and answer the questions.

1 Who are the characters in the picture?

2 What do you think Richard is thinking?

3 What do you think will happen to the young princes?

In a street in London in the year 1480 a small figure with a hunched [1] back was limping [2] towards the Tower of London. He appeared to be talking to himself.

'The long civil war between the houses of Lancaster and York is finally over,' he muttered, 'and peace has returned to England. My older brother, Edward, has become king, but I will not join in the celebrations.'

He paused and stared into the shadows.

'It is my bad luck to be ugly and deformed and because of this I will make everyone around me suffer most horribly. I cannot be a lover, so I will be a villain! And my first victim will be my own brother, Clarence! I have whispered words to Edward to make him suspicious of him.'

At that moment Clarence entered the street where Richard was standing. He was walking between two guards, and Richard smiled secretly. Clarence was being taken to the Tower of London and Richard's plans had already started to work. Richard limped towards Clarence and pretended to be sad.

'I will go to the king and do everything I can to set you free,' he said to Clarence. 'You won't be in prison for long. Be patient.' But when the guards led Clarence away he said to himself, 'I will make sure that Clarence never returns.

1. **hunched** : a back deformed by a hump.
2. **limping** : walking with difficulty because of an injured foot or leg.

The king is not well and he won't live long and, because Clarence is my older brother, he must die so that I become king. With Clarence out of the way I can turn my attention to Edward's sons.' Richard turned and thought for a moment. 'I need a queen, so my next plan is to marry Lady Anne Neville. I killed her husband and her father, but I'm sure I can persuade her to marry me.'

When Richard met her a little later that day, it was clear that Lady Anne despised Richard. She cursed [3] him as the murderer of her husband and his father, but Richard was clever.

'I didn't kill your husband,' he told her.

'Oh, then he must be alive,' replied Lady Anne sarcastically.

'Edward killed him,' said Richard.

'You're lying,' said Lady Anne.

'Oh, you are so clever, my lady. I cannot lie to you,' said Richard, and he paused as he looked into her eyes. 'Very well, I killed your husband, but your beauty was the cause.' Lady Anne stared at him in amazement as he told her that she should forgive him his crimes because he killed both her husband and her father out of love for her. Dramatically, Richard knelt before her and handed her his sword saying he would rather die than be hated by her. This was too much for Lady Anne. She could not kill him and, as she dropped the sword, Richard slipped a ring upon her finger.

'She hated me,' Richard said once she had gone, 'and I have used the power of words to win her. She has already forgotten her husband and I can see that she finds me attractive. Maybe I am not so ugly?' and Richard gave an evil laugh as he limped away.

At the palace, Queen Elizabeth, the wife of the very ill King Edward, was afraid. She knew that her two young sons, Prince Edward and Richard, the Duke of York, were too young to become king when her husband died and she knew that Richard would control the throne until the princes were old enough to rule. She knew that Richard hated her, and Queen Elizabeth feared for her life and the life of her children. It was while Elizabeth and Richard

---

3. **cursed** : spoke angrily (invoking for harm or punishment on someone).

were arguing that Queen Margaret, the old king's wife, stepped out of the shadows. 'You,' she said, pointing to Elizabeth, 'will live long, but you will not be a wife, a mother or a queen for long.' Then she turned to Richard. 'You will never sleep peacefully,' she said, 'because your friends are your enemies.' Then she left.

In the Tower of London, Clarence told his guard about a terrible dream he had had. He dreamt that he drowned [4] and in the underworld he saw the ghost of Prince Edward, Lady Anne's husband, who cursed him. The guard stayed with Clarence while he slept until two men arrived with papers signed by Richard allowing them to be alone with Clarence. The men were there on urgent business and their business was the murder of the future king of England. They had been paid by Richard to kill his brother. They seized Clarence and drowned him in a barrel of wine.

At the palace, King Edward seemed very weak and unwell, but he wanted everyone to make peace. He had sent a letter to the Tower of London forgiving his brother and when Elizabeth asked the guards to bring Clarence to the palace, Richard stepped forward.

'Everyone knows that the good Duke Clarence is dead,' Richard said.

'But I reversed the death sentence!' said the king.

'The poor man died by your first order,' replied Richard.

This was too much for the already weak king. Suffering from grief and guilt, King Edward died and Richard was made Lord Protector. It was agreed that he would rule until his oldest nephew, Prince Edward, was the right age to rule England alone. Queen Elizabeth was very afraid and she fled with her youngest son, Richard, to a church where the cardinal would give her sanctuary. When Richard heard this news he sent his faithful friend Buckingham to speak to the cardinal.

'Sanctuary is for those who need protection,' Buckingham said to the cardinal. 'I have heard of sanctuary for men, but not of sanctuary for children.'

---

4. **drowned** : died underwater.

The cardinal agreed. Richard took charge of the two young princes and told them that he would take them somewhere safe.

'Uncle Richard, where will I stay until my coronation?' asked the elder, Prince Edward.

'If I were you, I would stay in the Tower of London for a day or two,' replied Richard.

'I like most of the palaces, but I don't like the Tower of London,' said Prince Edward.

'I can't sleep quietly in the Tower,' said the younger.

'Why? What are you afraid of?' asked Richard.

'My uncle Clarence's angry ghost,' said the Duke of York. 'My grandmother told me he was murdered there.'

'I am not afraid of dead uncles,' said Edward.

'Or living ones, I hope,' said Richard.

'I hope not,' said the prince. 'I am not happy about this, but I will go to the Tower if this is what you want, Uncle Richard.'

Richard wanted to murder his two young nephews, but he was not sure that Hastings, a member of the court, would agree to his evil plan.

'Hastings loves the young princes as he loved their father. What will we do if he doesn't agree?' Buckingham asked Richard.

'Chop off his head,' replied Richard, and through a cunning plan Richard accused Hastings of treason and ordered his execution.

Fear was growing in the English court. Many people now realised that nothing could save England from Richard's mad desire for power.

The text and **beyond**

1 **Comprehension check**

For each question, mark the letter next to the correct answer — A, B, C or D.

1 The first person Richard plans to kill is

A ☐ Lady Anne.

B ☐ Edward IV.

C ☐ Clarence.

D ☐ Queen Elizabeth.

2 Richard tells Lady Anne that he killed her husband because

A ☐ Richard hated him.

B ☐ Richard hates Lady Anne.

C ☐ Richard loves Elizabeth.

D ☐ Richard loves Lady Anne.

3 Clarence dreams

A ☐ that two men murder him.

B ☐ that he drowns and sees a ghost.

C ☐ that he is taken to the Tower of London.

D ☐ that his guard murders him.

4 King Edward wants

A ☐ to forgive Clarence.

B ☐ to forgive Richard.

C ☐ to send Elizabeth to the Tower.

D ☐ to send the young princes to the Tower.

5 When King Edward dies

A ☐ Richard is crowned king.

B ☐ Prince Edward is crowned king.

C ☐ Richard is made Lord Protector.

D ☐ the Duke of York is made Lord Protector.

6 Hastings

A ☐ murders the two little princes.

B ☐ takes the princes to the Tower.

C ☐ kills Buckingham.

D ☐ is executed.

Richard was made Lord Protector.

Look at these sentences:

Hastings was executed.

Clarence was being taken to the Tower of London.

They had been paid by Richard.

These sentences are in the passive. We use the passive when the person or thing doing the action isn't important or isn't known. If we are using the passive and we want to say who did the action we use *by*. We form the passive by using the verb *be* in the correct form with the past participle of the main verb of the sentence.

Remember: only verbs that have an object can have a passive form. When verbs have two objects, we usually use the person as the subject.

ACTIVE	PASSIVE 1	PASSIVE 2
They offered a job to Bob. →	*A job was offered to Bob.* →	*Bob was offered a job.*

2 The passive
Change the following sentences from active to passive.

1   Richard slipped a ring on Lady Anne's finger.

2   Two men drowned Clarence in a barrel of wine.

3   King Edward sent a letter to the Tower of London forgiving his brother.

4   Richard took the princes to the Tower of London.

5   Richard sent his friend Buckingham to speak to the cardinal.

6   Richard used a cunning plan to accuse Hastings of treason.

3 Vocabulary
Find the word that does not belong with the other three words and then explain why.

1   murder/assassinate/die/kill

2   cunning/crafty/deceitful/mad

3   ran away/feared/fled/escaped

4   comfort/grief/misery/unhappiness

5   lie/joke/deceive/trick

6   quietly/quickly/peacefully/calmly

7   agree/argue/quarrel/row

FCE **4** **The Tower of London**

Read the text below and think of the word which best fits each space. Use only one word for each space. There is an example at the beginning (0).

The Tower of London is well known for (**0**) ....its................ history of gunpowder, treason, imprisonment and murder. It is the oldest royal castle (**1**) .... Europe and it is closely linked (**2**) .... the history of London.

William the Conqueror wanted a fortress outside the city of London and so he built what is now called the White Tower in 1078. In 1240, Henry II painted the tower white and it became (**3**) .... as Julius Caesar's Tower.

For centuries the Tower (**4**) .... used to hold important prisoners. Prisoners entered (**5**) .... boat through Traitors Gate. Some were beheaded and many were (**6**) .... seen again. Two of the most famous prisoners were the little princes, twelve-year-old Edward and his nine-year-old brother Richard. They were sent there by their uncle, the Duke of Gloucester, and (**7**) .... the little princes were seen playing in the gardens (**8**) .... June 1483, in July Richard declared that they were illegitimate and they were never seen again.

In 1647 the skeletons of two children (**9**) .... found when a building to the south (**10**) .... the White Tower was demolished. King Charles II said they were the princes and had their bones buried at Westminster Abbey.

By the time Elizabeth I came to (**11**) .... throne, there were twenty towers and there was a wide deep moat. The Wakefield Tower is (**12**) .... the crown jewels are kept. The jewels include St. Edward's Crown, which has been used at the coronations of all the kings and queens since Charles II.

T: GRADE 8

5 **Speaking – Personal values and ideals**

Richard III is one of the most determined literary figures. He wants to become king and will achieve it at any price. Ask and answer the questions.

1 Personal values are the guidelines that we live and work by daily, but do we all have the same values?

2 What does it mean acting in a moral manner?

3 Can personal ideals make us ruthless?

4 Can a person who isn't prepared to be ruthless get to the top of their profession?

5 What are the personal values that you live by?

6 What are your ideals?

▶▶▶ **INTERNET** PROJECT ◀◀◀

Films based on Shakespeare's plays

There are many film versions of Shakespeare's plays. *Looking for Richard* is a film which shows rehearsals for *Richard III* together with interview with actors. Connect to the Internet and find more information about this film. Then answer the following questions.

1 When was the film made?

2 Who directed it?

3 Who played Lady Anne?

Ian Mckellen played Richard in a film directed by Richard Loncraine in 1995. Find out more information on the Internet about the film. Then decide if the sentences are T (true) or F (false).

		T	F
1	This film version was set in 16th century Britain.	☐	☐
2	The film wasn't nominated for any Oscars.	☐	☐
3	Kristin Scott Thomas played Lady Anne.	☐	☐
4	The film went on general release on 19th January 1996.	☐	☐
5	Richard Loncraine, the director, is a theatre director.	☐	☐
6	The film is a very cinematic adaptation.	☐	☐

Before you read

1 Vocabulary

Match the words (1-5) to the pictures (A-E).

1 crown   **2** tent   **3** drum   **4** sword   **5** prison

A☐   B☐   C☐   D☐   E☐

2 Reading pictures

Look at the pictures on page 23. Answer the questions.

1 Where is Richard?

2 Why does he look so afraid?

3 Who can Richard see in his dreams?

4 What do you think they are saying to Richard?

3 Listening

Read the first part of Part Two. You will hear a conversation between Richard and Buckingham. For questions 1-7, complete the sentences.

The people of London did not **(1)** .... the rumours Richard and Buckingham were spreading.

The people loved the little **(2)** ....

They would not shout 'God save Richard, England's loyal
(3) .... !'

Richard planned that he would not show any desire for the
(4) ....

Richard did not feel secure with the young princes still **(5)** .... in the Tower.

Richard wanted to **(6)** .... Buckingham.

'I want my **(7)** .... murdered,' Richard said.

Richard's plans moved quickly, with Buckingham as his right-hand man. 5 @ Mp3
He persuaded Buckingham to tell as many people as he could that King
Edward had been an illegitimate child. Buckingham spread rumours around
the streets of London that the princes were illegitimate too. Buckingham
also told the Lord Mayor of London that Hastings had been plotting to kill
Richard and this was why he had been executed. The Lord Mayor told
Richard that he would tell the people of London what a dangerous traitor
Hastings had been, but the common people did not believe this. They knew
that it was all lies invented by Richard and the citizens of London loved the
young princes.

When Buckingham returned, Richard asked, 'So, what did the people say?'

'They stood like silent statues and did not say a word,' replied Buckingham.

'Did you tell them that Edward's children are illegitimate?' asked Richard.

'I did. I asked them to shout "God save Richard, England's loyal king!"'

'And did they?' asked Richard.

'No, they didn't say a word,' replied Buckingham, 'but we must proceed
with our idea and persuade the Lord Mayor that the people want you to be
king.'

---

5. **right-hand man** : a person's most trusted helper.

19

Their plan worked and later, when the Lord Mayor asked Richard, he pretended that he did not want to be king.

'The people want you as their king,' said the Lord Mayor.

'I cannot. I am not worthy of such a great honour,' replied Richard.

Reluctantly, Richard accepted the crown and he and his new wife, Lady Anne, were crowned the next day. Richard was king at last and, although he was very pleased about this, he did not feel secure with the young princes still alive in the Tower.

'Oh, Buckingham, now I'm going to test you. The young princes in the Tower are still alive. What do you think I'm going to say next?'

'I don't know,' replied Buckingham.

'I want my nephews murdered. Do I have your permission to kill them?' Richard asked Buckingham, but his loyal right-hand man became cold and pale. 'I'll let you know my answer soon,' Buckingham said, and he left the room.

'You're too weak to be my right-hand man,' Richard murmured, and then he spoke to a man called Tyrell, who agreed to kill the princes for a large fee. Richard was delighted when Tyrell returned to the palace with the news that the two young princes were dead.

Richard spread rumours that Queen Anne was ill and about to die. He gave orders to keep the queen locked in her room and later poisoned her. He rubbed [6] his hands with delight. 'Clarence's daughter is married to an unimportant man and his son is in prison. My wife, Queen Anne, is dead and now I want to marry my brother Edward's young daughter, Elizabeth.'

But there was bad news from France. Richard's noblemen were leaving to join Richmond, a descendent of the Lancaster family, in France. Richmond was preparing to fight Richard for the throne of England. Richard knew that he had to gather his own army and meet Richmond in battle.

In the palace Richard's mother, the Duchess of York, and Elizabeth cried when they heard that the young princes were dead.

'Richard, you arrived on earth to make my life hell,' said the duchess.

---

6. **rubbed** : moved one hand against the other.

'Now listen just this once and I will never speak to you again.'

'Alright,' said Richard.

'I pray that the souls of Edward's children will whisper to your enemies and promise them success and victory,' said the duchess. 'You are violent and your end will be violent.'

'I agree with everything your mother said,' added Queen Elizabeth.

'Wait, madam,' said Richard to Elizabeth. 'I need to speak to you.'

'What do you want to speak about?' she said. 'I have no more royal sons for you to murder.'

'You have a beautiful daughter called Elizabeth,' said Richard.

Elizabeth didn't know, but Richard wanted to marry her daughter.

'How can I show my love for her?' Richard asked Elizabeth.

'You can send her the bloody hearts of her two little brothers. Write "Edward" and "York" on them. That might win her love,' replied Elizabeth coldly. 'You can tell her about all the people you have murdered... her uncles, Clarence and Rivers, and her good aunt, Anne.'

'This marriage is the only way that we can avoid civil war,' Richard insisted. Even though Elizabeth hated him, she said that she would speak to her daughter about his offer of marriage.

Reports arrived at the palace saying that Richmond had reached England with a fleet of ships. When Richard heard that all over Britain noblemen were prepared to join Richmond, he began to panic. Buckingham was now terrified of Richard and he escaped.

'Capture him,' Richard ordered. Buckingham was quickly taken by the few men still loyal to Richard and executed.

When Richard heard the news that Richmond was in the centre of England, near Leicester, he led his army to Bosworth. 'Let's put our tents up here in Bosworth Field and beat these rebels at home.'

Richard ordered his men to prepare their tents for the night. They would fight against Richmond the next morning. Richard slept, but he had a terrible nightmare. The ghosts of everyone he had murdered came to visit him. Eleven ghosts, among them King Henry IV, Edward and Clarence, Richard's brothers, the two princes, his wife Lady Anne and Buckingham cursed him and told him that he would die in the battle the next day. Then the ghosts moved on and spoke to sleeping Richmond. They told him that he would rule England and be the father of a race of kings.

Richard woke terrified from the dream. He was sweating and gasping, and for the first time he was really afraid. He searched his soul to find the cause for such a dream.

'What am I afraid of?' he asked himself. 'Am I afraid of myself? There's no one else here. Is there a murderer here? No...Yes, I am.'

Suddenly Richard realised what he had done.

In his camp Richmond woke and told his advisors about his dream, which was full of good omens [7] for the battle. In a battle speech to his soldiers Richmond told them that they were defending their country from a tyrant and a murderer.

'Listen!' Richmond said to his soldiers. 'I hear the drums. Fight, gentlemen of England!'

Then the two armies fought. News arrived to Richmond saying that Richard's horse had been killed and that he was fighting like a madman on foot. Richmond searched for Richard and they fought until Richard lay dead on the battlefield.

Richmond became King of England and announced his decision to marry Elizabeth, daughter of the late King Edward. Finally, the two houses of York and Lancaster were united.

---

7. **omens** : signs of what will happen in the future.

The text and **beyond**

1 Comprehension check

Read the text below and decide wich answer (A, B, C or D) best fits each space (1-10). There is an example at the beginning (0).

The Real Richard III

Some people do not think that Richard was (**0**) ...D..... power-driven man Shakespeare portrays in his play. The stories of Richard's evil only began after his death. There is (**1**) .... written about his physical deformity in (**2**) .... documents. His portraits show a normal man.

Richard did good deeds during his reign. He was successful in defending England from the Scots, and he improved the living standards of the common (**3**) ....

(**4**) ...., the accusations and mystery surrounding the murder of the princes 5) .... linger.

There is (**6**) .... mystery.

At Bosworth Field, in 1485, Richard had a bigger army than Richmond, but yet he was defeated and he was the last English king to die on the battlefield. (**7**) .... knows what happened to Richard's body. Three skulls (**8**) .... in the river, but it is not (**9**) .... if one of them is Richard's. Richard was, and still (**10**) .... to this day, an enigma.

RICARDVS · III · ANG · REX ·

0	**A** An	**B** a	**C** /	**D** the
1	**A** something	**B** anything	**C** nothing	**D** everything
2	**A** some	**B** any	**C** the	**D** a
3	**A** men	**B** person	**C** persons	**D** people
4	**A** Despite	**B** However	**C** In spite of	**D** How
5	**A** still	**B** again	**C** more	**D** yet
6	**A** other	**B** yet	**C** again	**D** another
7	**A** Nothing	**B** Everywhere	**C** Something	**D** No one
8	**A** were found	**B** was found	**C** has been found	**D** will find
9	**A** know	**B** been known	**C** known	**D** knowing
10	**A** stay	**B** rest	**C** be	**D** remains

2 Vocabulary

Complete the summary of *Richard III*. Choose words from the list. There are some extra words that you don't need.

> ill   castle   nephew   murderer   curse   niece   evil   villain
> unite   murdered   gathers   throne   crowned   civil   physical
> world   peace   heirs   wit   mental   blames

The long (1) .... war between the houses of York and Lancaster is over and finally there is (2) .... in England. King Edward IV is on the (3) ...., but his younger brother Richard is hungry for power. Because of his (4) .... deformity, he cannot be a lover and so he decides to be a (5) .... and kill anyone who stands between him and the throne of England. His plan begins.
He has his older brother, Clarence, (6) .... and then (7) .... the king for Clarence's death. Using intelligence, (8) .... and passion he persuades Lady Anne to marry him, even though he killed her husband. When the (9) .... king dies, Richard puts the two little princes and rightful (10) .... to the throne in the Tower of London. Later Richard hires a (11) .... to kill the little princes. The people of England hate Richard and no one is happy when he is (12) .... king. In order to make his claim to the throne stronger, he decides to marry his (13) .... Elizabeth and so he has Lady Anne murdered.
Richmond, a descendent of the Lancaster family, (14) .... a large army and prepares to fight Richard, but on the night before the battle Richard has a terrible dream. All the people he has murdered appear and (15) .... him.
The following morning Richard is killed in battle. Richmond is crowned King Henry VII and marries Elizabeth, uniting the houses of York and Lancaster.

3 Synonyms

A synonym is a word that has the same or almost the same meaning as another word. For each sentence, substitute the underlined word with the synonym you will find in the box.

> oppression   indecisive   news   motive   payment   escape   ready

1   Your beauty was the <u>cause</u>.
2   You are too <u>weak</u> to be my right-hand man.
3   Tyrell agreed to kill the princes for a large <u>fee</u>.
4   I am not <u>fit</u> to rule.
5   <u>Reports</u> arrived at the palace saying that Richmond had reached England with a fleet of ships.
6   This marriage is the only way we can <u>avoid</u> civil war.
7   Buckingham escaped fearing Richard's <u>tyranny</u>.

4 Characters

Answer the questions with the name of one of the characters from the story.

Who...

1 told Richard he was violent and his end would be violent? ....

2 told his advisors about his dream full of good omens? ....

3 would not agree to Richard's plan to murder the princes? ....

4 did not like the Tower of London? ....

5 suffered from grief and guilt over Clarence's execution? ....

6 had a dream about drowning? ....

7 hated Richard but could not kill him? ....

FCE 5 Writing

You have decided to enter a short story competition. The rules say that your story must begin with the following sentences.

> *Uncle Richard's castle looked dark and frightening. I wondered what a weekend staying with him would be like. The door opened and...*

Write your story for the competition. (120-180 words)

6 Speaking – the 'hot seat'

A chair in front of the class is the 'hot seat'. While you are sitting in this chair, you are either **Richard, Lady Anne** or **Buckingham**. The people pretending to be Richard, Lady Anne or Buckingham should try to be as accurate as possible, but they will also have to invent things and interpret things themselves. Take turns sitting there. The rest of the class can ask the person in the hot seat any questions. Below are some examples.

Questions for Richard

1 How could you kill your brother Clarence? Did you hate him so much?

2 Why did you marry Lady Anne? Did you ever love her?

3 Why is being king so important to you, that you would kill your family and friends?

Questions for Lady Anne

1 Richard killed your husband and your father. Why did you marry him?

2 Why did you not try to kill Richard?

3 What was it like being married to Richard?

Questions for Buckingham

1 Why did you become a close friend of Richard when you knew what he was capable of doing?

2 Was Richard a good friend?

3 How did you feel when he put the little princes in the Tower?

Scene from an Open Air Theatre production of *Hamlet* (1994).

The Influences on
Shakespeare's Plays

Shakespeare's work was strongly influenced by the politics and philosophy of his times as well as the thinkers and writers of ancient cultures.

Queen Elizabeth I had been on the throne for six years when Shakespeare was born and she ruled for most of his working life. The stage had a powerful friend in Elizabeth. The aristocracy were granted licences for the maintenance of actors and Queen Elizabeth's Men were a company of actors formed in 1583 at the request of the Queen. Altogether there were about twenty playing companies at that time and about fifteen theatres.

Without Elizabeth's support, the plays of William Shakespeare's plays may never have been written. In Renaissance England poets and playwrights needed patrons to support their work. Queen Elizabeth was a theatre lover and Shakespeare and his company played before her many times.

The Armada Portrait (about 1588) by George Gower.

Elizabeth, who was a wise leader, certainly influenced Shakespeare when he was creating his strong female characters. Some scholars think that, despite the patriarchal time period in which he wrote, there are plenty of strong unconventional female characters in his works. Shakespeare had an exceptional insight into human behaviour and he portrayed the situation of women in a patriarchal society through examples of women in power. Sometimes these women seem to be treated with mistrust by Shakespeare. Gertude in *Hamlet*, marries her brother-in-law and her husband's murderer and Lady Macbeth urges her husband to kill the king. In the end these strong women die.

James I (1566-1625) is seen as another influential patron in Shakespeare's life. He probably wrote *Macbeth* (1606) for James I. Many people think Duncan's murder in the play connects with the Gunpowder Plot of 1605. This happened because James I wasn't very tolerant of the Catholics in England. So, on 5th November 1605 when King James I was due to open Parliament, thirteen Catholics decided

Detail from John de Critz the Elder's portrait of King James I (1566-1625).

to blow up the Houses of Parliament. The plot failed and Guy Fawkes, one of the plotters, was executed, but people were shocked that anyone should try to kill the king.

Shakespeare dramatised history from many different periods because it had a didactic function. In fact, the popular appeal of his plays stirred patriotic feeling and a new historical consciousness.

Shakespeare's plays are divided into cycles according to the periods of history they refer to. There are:

- the Greek Cycle: *Troilus and Cressida, Timon of Athens*.
- the Roman Cycle: *Coriolanus, Julius Caesar, Anthony and Cleopatra* and *Titus Andronicus*.
- the Celtic Cycle: *Cymbeline, King Lear, Hamlet* and *Macbeth*.
- the Wars of the Roses Cycle: *Richard II, Henry IV* 1 and 2, *Henry V, Henry VI* part 1, 2, 3 and *Richard III*.

Greek and Roman classics were popular in the Renaissance and inspired Shakespeare's writing. Shakespeare was a sophisticated reader of Ovid, his favourite Roman poet. Shakespeare's representation of mythology and metamorphosis were influenced by his works.

Another important source of inspiration for Shakespeare was Nicolò Machiavelli. Nicolò Machiavelli, an Italian statesman and political philosopher, was born in Florence in 1469. His contact with Cesare Borgia, the son of Pope Alexander VI and a ruthless statesman, provided him with material for his writing and in his most famous work, *Il principe* (*The Prince*, 1532) in which he explained how a

Portrait of Nicolò Machiavelli
by Santi di Tito (1536-1606).

prince could set out to gain absolute power and how he could keep it. Machiavelli believed that weakness in a man revealed a defect in his personality and prevented him from making the right decisions when he was seeking power.

Shakespeare's England socially and politically had similarities with Florence in the first part of the century. England was an autocratic state and there was always the fear of conspiracy. Shakespeare may not have read Machiavelli, but he saw Machiavel characters in the theatre. Christopher Marlowe created a Machiavel character in *The Jew of Malta* (1592).

There are Machiavel characters in many Shakespearean plays, for example Iago in *Othello*, Edmund in *King Lear*, and Richard III. Shakespeare also created Claudius, who murders his brother for the throne of Denmark, and even Henry V shows Machiavel decisiveness. However, Shakespeare's greatest study of the effects of human ambition and the forces of evil, might be in the characters of Macbeth and his wife and Richard III. Both plays reflect on the terrible consequences of unchecked ambition and power.

1 Comprehension check

Answer the following questions.

1 What were Shakespeare's main influences?
2 What was Queen Elizabeth I's attitude towards Shakespeare's plays?
3 Which Roman poet influenced Shakespeare, and how?
4 How did Machiavelli influence Shakespeare?
5 Name some of Shakespeare's Machiavel characters.

Before you read

1 Look at the list of characters in the story before you start reading.

King Henry V: young King of England
the Archbishop of Canterbury and the Bishop of Ely: wealthy and powerful English clergymen
the Dauphin: son of the King of France
Bardolph, Pistol, Nym: commoners and friends of Henry in his youth
the Duke of Exeter: Henry's uncle and a military leader
Katharine: the French king's daughter
King Charles VI: the King of France
Montjoy: a French messenger
Williams: a soldier

Setting: London and the battlefields of Harfleur and Agincourt, in France, around 1414-1415.

2 **Listening**

Listen to the beginning of Part One. You will hear clergymen discussing the change in Henry, the new King of England, and their advice to him. For questions 1-7, complete the sentences.

Henry used to be called (**1**) ....

England and France have been at war for (**2**) .... years.

Henry has changed. He is now virtuous and (**3**) ....

The bishops will give Henry (**4**) .... for the war.

The Archbishop advises Henry to (**5**) ....

The Dauphin sends Henry a box of (**6**) ....

Henry begins to prepare for (**7**) .... against France.

3 **Vocabulary**

Match a word in A with a definition in B. Use your dictionary if necessary.

A		B	
1	commoner	A	where bees live
2	claim	B	a secret plan
3	beehive	C	a person who isn't noble
4	virtuous	D	a statute, not yet made law
5	bill	E	a right to something
6	plot	F	morally excellent

Times were hard in England and King Henry IV was dead. His son Prince Hal  or Harry was on the throne and, now that he was king, everyone called him Henry. Prince Hal was a wild young boy. He was always with his friends at the Boar's Head Inn and mixing with commoners, but his responsibility as King of England had changed him. It was a difficult time to be king. England and France had been at war for twenty-five years. Finally there was peace, but everyone knew that it wouldn't last. The French would certainly sail across the sea if they thought that England had a weak young king. Henry knew that he had to be a strong king!

In a room in the king's palace in London, the Archbishop of Canterbury and the Bishop of Ely were discussing a parliamentary bill. The bill would take half of the church's land and wealth. The money would go to the army, the poor and to the king.

'What can we do to stop this?' said the Bishop of Ely.

'Henry is very different now. He is virtuous and intelligent,' said the Archbishop of Canterbury. 'He wasn't like this when he was younger. He preferred banquets and sport then,' said the Bishop of Ely.

'This change to his character is a miracle,' said the Archbishop of Canterbury. 'King Henry believes that he can be King of France too. War with France would help him to forget this bill. I'll give him money from the church to help with the war.'

'The French ambassadors are here,' said the Bishop of Ely.

'Let's go to the throne room and hear what they have to say,' replied the Archbishop of Canterbury.

'Welcome, Archbishop,' said Henry. 'I need you to explain why I have a claim to the throne of France. Give me your honest opinion and your advice.'

'In France,' explained the Archbishop, 'there is a law called the Salic law. If a king has a daughter, the daughter's son cannot become king. This law doesn't exist in England. In England kings can inherit the throne through a female relative. King Henry, your great-great-grandmother was a daughter of the King of France. Under English law, you are the true heir to the throne of France. Of course the French don't agree. They believe that their king, Charles VI, is the true king. My advice is to fight.'

Henry's advisors agreed with the Archbishop of Canterbury, but Henry was worried about problems at home. 'The Scottish rebels could be a danger while I'm away.'

'Divide your kingdom like a beehive,' said the Archbishop. 'Take one quarter of your army and leave the others here to defend England.'

Henry agreed, and called the French ambassadors into the room.

'The Dauphin, the son of the King of France, laughs at your claim to the French throne. He says that you are too young for that responsibility,' said the first ambassador. 'The Dauphin has sent you a present.'

It was a box of tennis balls.

'A joke!' Henry said angrily. 'Thank the Dauphin for the present. Tell him that I will go to France and play a great match. And I won't play this match with tennis balls, but with cannon balls!'

The French ambassadors left and Henry began to prepare for war against France. Young men left their farms and joined the king's army and the French were afraid. There was even a plot to kill Henry before he sailed for France, but the plot failed.

Outside the Boar's Head Tavern, in London, Henry's old friends, Bardolph, Pistol and Nym met, but they too were preparing to leave for war.

'Good to see you, Corporal Nym,' said Bardolph.

'Good morning, Lieutenant Bardolph,' replied Nym.

'That's a fine sword you have, Nym.'

'It's just a simple sword, but I can cook cheese on the fire with it,' said Nym. The friends laughed and left for France.

In his palace in Rouen, the King of France received news of Henry's progress. 'We must be courageous as we prepare for war. We need strong men who can defend our country,' he said.

'It will be easy to defeat the English,' said his son. 'Henry is vain.'

'Don't misjudge the character of King Henry. Remember that his relatives were Edward III and his son, the Black Prince, who beat us at the Battle of Crécy,' said King Charles.

At that moment the Duke of Exeter, Henry's uncle and a trusted advisor, arrived with a message from Henry. 'King Henry asks you for the crown of France. If you don't give it to him, there will be war. King Henry did not like the gift of tennis balls and soon you will have to apologise.'

'He wants me to surrender,' said Charles. 'Tell King Henry that I will give him my answer tomorrow.'

Henry did not wait in England to hear the French king's answer. He landed with his warships at Harfleur, on the northern coast of France. Then news arrived from the French palace. King Charles VI of France offered Henry his beautiful daughter Katharine, but he said that he would not give up the throne of France. King Henry rejected Charles's offer and prepared to fight.

Henry's army had been attacking the walls of Harfleur without success. Henry knew that he would have to speak to his army. Outside the city walls Henry gave a passionate speech.

'Attack the city walls again, dear friends! When the battle trumpets sound in our ears, then it is time to act like a tiger. Tense your muscles and with eyes shining, take a deep breath. On, on noble Englishmen! Make your fathers proud as you lift your swords. Follow your spirit into battle and shout "God for Henry, England and Saint George!"'

King Henry's former friends were outside the walls of Harfleur. 'On, on,' shouted Bardolph. He was inspired by Henry's speech. He wanted to run up to the city walls and attack, but Nym and Pistol reminded him that he could be killed.

'Please, Corporal, stop. The fighting is too violent,' said Nym. 'I have only one life, not twelve.'

'I wish I was back in the tavern in London,' said Pistol.

They were a strange group. Bardolph looked strong, but he was a coward. Pistol spoke a lot, but he didn't use his sword. Nym and Bardolph were brothers in crime. They stole gloves and handkerchiefs from men's pockets. All three were terrified about the thought of death.

The English soldiers were busy digging a tunnel under the walls of Harfleur when suddenly trumpets sounded. The citizens of Harfleur wanted to negotiate. The governor of the town appeared on the wall and Henry spoke to him.

'Surrender now,' Henry threatened 'and the people of your town will be allowed to live. Terrible things will happen if you do not surrender.'

'Today our hopes are at an end,' replied the governor. 'A messenger came from the Dauphin saying that he cannot send an army. So, great King, we surrender our town and lives to your mercy.'

'Open your gates,' said Henry.

Henry left his uncle, the Duke of Exeter, in charge of the town of Harfleur and led the army to Calais.

The text and **beyond**

FCE 1 Comprehension check

For each question, mark the letter next to the correct answer A, B, C or D.

1 If a parliamentary bill is passed
  A ☐ there will be war with France.
  B ☐ half of the church's land and wealth will go to the army, the poor and the king.
  C ☐ the French will sail across the sea.
  D ☐ money will not go to the poor.

2 In France Salic law means that
  A ☐ kings can inherit the throne through a female relative.
  B ☐ kings can inherit the throne through a male relative.
  C ☐ a foreigner can never be king.
  D ☐ a foreigner can be king.

3 The French king thought that
  A ☐ Henry would send the Black Prince.
  B ☐ Henry's relatives would help.
  C ☐ it would be easy to defeat the English.
  D ☐ it might not be easy to defeat the English.

4 The French king offered Henry
  A ☐ his palace.
  B ☐ his wife.
  C ☐ his daughter.
  D ☐ the Dauphin.

5 Henry spoke to his army outside Harfleur and said
  A ☐ 'Let every soldier blow his trumpet!'
  B ☐ 'Let the tigers loose!'
  C ☐ 'Let's go home!'
  D ☐ 'Let's attack the city walls!'

6 The governor of Harfleur said
  A ☐ the Dauphin would not send an army.
  B ☐ the Dauphin would send an army.
  C ☐ the Dauphin wanted to negotiate.
  D ☐ the Dauphin didn't want to negotiate.

2 Vocabulary

A Complete the table.

Verb	Noun	Adjective
explain	....	explainable
....	advice	advisable
prepare	....	preparatory
agree	....	agreeable
apologise	....	apologetic
....	reminder	reminiscent
inspire	inspiration	....

B For questions 1-6, read the text below. Use the word given in capitals at the end of some of the lines to form a word that fits in the gap in the same line. There is an example at the beginning (0)

Henry needed an (0) ...explanation... about French law and so he   **EXPLAIN**
asked the (1) .... of the Archbishop of Canterbury and   **ADVISE**
the Bishop of Ely.

'Take one quarter of your army and leave the others to defend
England,' they said. Henry was in complete (2) ....   **AGREE**
He began (3) .... for war at once.   **PREPARE**

The Duke of Exeter (4) .... the French King that Henry   **REMIND**
wanted an (5) .... over the Dauphin's gift of tennis balls.   **APOLOGISE**

When the English reached France, Henry gave an (6) ....   **INSPIRE**
speech to his army.

That's the king who is very different now.

In defining relative clauses, the relative clause identifies the person (*who, that*), thing (*which, that*), place (*where*), time (*when*) or reason (*why*) we are referring to. *That* can be used instead of *who* or *which*.

This is a law which/that doesn't exist in England.

The relative pronoun can be left out if it is the object of the verb in the relative clause.

Example: *The woman (who/that) I spoke to on the phone last week told me the museum would be open.*

No commas are used before or after the relative clause.

3 Defining relative clauses

Join a clause in column A to a clause in column B with an appropriate relative pronoun to make a complete sentence.

A		B	
1 ☐ France is the place		**A**	King Henry's old friends met.
2 ☐ The Dauphin is the person		**B**	the Dauphin sent me.
3 ☐ The Black Prince is the relative		**C**	there was the Salic law.
4 ☐ The Boar's Head Tavern is		**D**	laughs at Henry's claim on the French throne.
5 ☐ These are the tennis balls		**E**	beat the French at the battle of Crécy.

'We must prepare for war with men of courage, who can defend our country,' said the king.

The relative pronouns *who*, *which*, *where* and *whose* are used to make non-defining relative clauses. We use *who* for people, *which* for things, *where* for place and *whose* for possessions. We cannot replace them with *that* and we cannot omit them. The non-defining relative clause gives extra information, which can be left out. It isn't essential to understanding the meaning of the sentence, but it tells us more. We use commas before and after the relative clause.

Example: *My brother, who is older than me, is going to university in September.*

London, where I lived for five years, has become very expensive.

We use relative pronouns to link sentences.

Example: *Thank you for the Birthday card. I got it yesterday.*

Thank you for the birthday card, which I got yesterday.

4 Non-defining relative clauses

Match sentences 1-6 with sentences A-F. Use relative pronouns to make each pair of sentences into one sentence.

1 ☐ Prince Hal was a wild young boy
2 ☐ 'Let's go to the throne room
3 ☐ The king wants to pass a parliamentary bill
4 ☐ It will be easy to defeat the English
5 ☐ Henry spoke to his army
6 ☐ King Henry has relatives

A …….. beat the French at the Battle of Crécy.
B …….. king is a vain man.
C …….. the king is waiting for us.'
D …….. was outside the city of Harfleur.
E …….. was always drinking with his friends.
F …….. will take half the church's land and wealth.

5 **Speaking – Early memories**

King Henry was called Prince Hal when he was young and he had a lot of freedom.
What are your early memories? You can bring in a photo to help you speak.

1   What did you look like when you were a child?

2   What were you like? Shy/extrovert?

3   Did you have a favourite toy? Which toy?

4   What are your memories of your home?

5   What did you enjoy doing?

6   Did you have a best friend? Who?

6 **Characters**

A   Complete the sentences about the characters in Part One. Choose a character
adjective and a suitable reason from the following lists. There are some extra
adjectives that you don't need.

Character adjectives

wild   brave   virtuous   strong   afraid   coward   talkative   worried

Reasons

- the fighting was violent
- responsibility had changed him
- they didn't want to die
- he needed to defend his country

1   King Henry was .... because ....

2   The French king was .... because ....

3   The English soldiers were .... because ....

4   Bardolph, Pistol and Nym were .... because ....

B   Write four more sentences about the same characters. Use the remaining
adjectives in List A and invent a suitable reason to explain your choice.

1   ....

2   ....

3   ....

4   ....

7 Map work: Henry's campaign

Look at the map of Henry's first campaign in France and answer the questions.

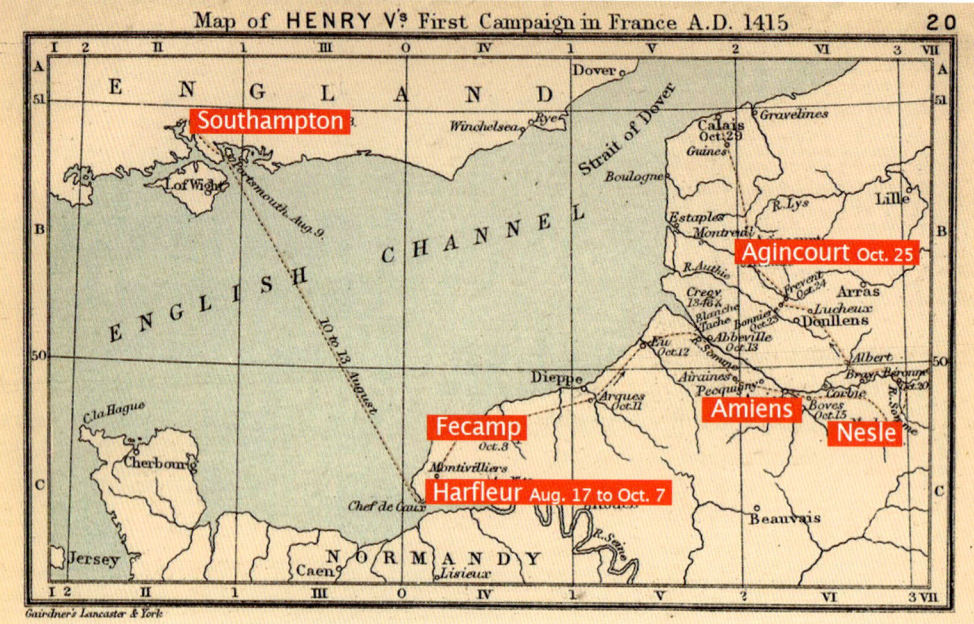

1 Which port did Henry sail from?

2 Where did they land in France?

3 How long did they stay in Harfleur?

4 Which route did they take to Agincourt?

5 When did they arrive?

8 Harfleur

Read the text about Harfleur and choose the correct alternative.

When Henry (**1**) *put/set* sail for France, the French army decided (**2**) *staying/to stay* just south of Calais and wait. They were certain that Henry could not capture the city of Harfleur. On the southern (**3**) *side/place* of the city was the River Lezarde. There (**4**) *were/was* salt marshes (**5**) *by/in* the east, with only a (**6**) *single/one* road. A wall ran all around the city with only three gates and the fact that there was a moat (**7**) *meaned/meant* that the city was surrounded (**8**) *by/in* water. Henry's men fired (**9**) *they're/their* cannons at the city walls (**10**) *for/in* two months and on Sunday 22nd September the city surrendered.

Before you read

1 Reading pictures

Look at the picture on page 47 and answer the questions.

1   What is this picture of?
2   How do we know that Henry is fighting here?
3   How are the two soldiers protected?
4   What do you think will happen?

2 Prediction

What do you think will happen next? Put a tick (✓) in the boxes.

1   ☐   Katharine refuses to marry Henry.
2   ☐   The English soldiers are worried about the battle.
3   ☐   The English army surrender before the battle.
4   ☐   The French army are not confident.
5   ☐   Henry orders his soldiers to kill all the French prisoners.
6   ☐   Henry worries constantly about the safety of England.

Read Part Two and check your ideas.

3 Listening

Listen to the first part of Part Two. In the French palace in Rouen, where the king's daughter Katharine is, the French king's advisors are speaking about Henry's progress. For questions 1-8 complete the sentences.

Katharine is learning **(1)** ....

A French advisor said that the English live in a **(2)** ...., cold, dark climate.

The French king will not let the Dauphin **(3)** .... Henry crossed the Somme River with his **(4)** ....

Henry would punish his soldiers with **(5)** .... if they **(6)** .... from French villages.

Montjoy says that the French army were only **(7)** .... He called King Henry **(8)** .... and foolish.

In the palace in Rouen, Katharine, the king's daughter, was learning English. She knew that soon she would need to speak to the King of England. In another part of the palace, King Charles was speaking to his advisors.

'Henry has crossed the Somme River,' said Charles.

'The English are braver than we thought,' said one advisor. 'They live in a foggy, cold, dark climate.'

'Stop King Henry and bring him to Rouen as our prisoner,' said the French king. The French nobility came to fight against the English, but Charles commanded the Dauphin to stay with him. 'Bring us news of England's defeat,' he said.

Henry crossed the Somme River with his army and came to a field in northern France, near a fort called Agincourt. Bardolph had been caught stealing in Harfleur. Henry had said that the punishment was death for anyone caught looting and, although Bardolph had been a friend of Henry's when he was a prince, Henry would not forgive him. 'I agree with this punishment. English soldiers mustn't steal from French villages.'

A fanfare sounded announcing the arrival of Montjoy, a French messenger. He had a message from the King of France. 'Tell Henry of

England that though we seemed dead, we were only asleep. The King of England will soon discover how weak and foolish he is.'

'My army is small and tired,' replied Henry 'but if we have to, we will fight.'

Firelight burned in the French and English camps and the horses stamped [1] their feet and called to each other. The French army were confident. They thought that it would be an easy victory because there were five Frenchmen to every one Englishman. The English soldiers were sure that they were going to die. Henry moved around the camp giving words of encouragement to his soldiers. He called his soldiers "brothers" and they were pleased to see the king that they called "Harry in the night".

King Henry was worried about the battle. He wanted to know what the soldiers really thought of him. So he borrowed an old brown cloak and pretended to be an ordinary soldier. He moved from campfire to campfire talking to the soldiers. Some said that they doubted the motives and courage of the king. Henry tried to defend the king, but a soldier called Williams could not agree. Williams and the disguised Henry exchanged gloves. They would fight if they both survived the battle.

When the soldiers left, Henry sat and thought about the responsibilities of being king. 'An ordinary man can enjoy his country's peace. He can sleep at night and doesn't have to worry about the safety of England.'

It was nearly dawn and almost time for the battle.

In the English camp Henry spoke to his soldiers.

'If anyone doesn't want to fight, then leave. Today is the feast of St. Crispin. The soldiers who survive the battle will stand proud, when people speak of this day. They'll roll up their shirts and show their scars. Old men forget, but you will remember every detail of what you did today. We few, we happy few, we band of brothers — for whoever sheds his blood with me today shall be my brother. However humble your birth is, this day will give you nobility and men back in England will curse themselves for not having been here and think less of themselves when they listen to the stories of those who fought with us on St. Crispin's Day.'

---

1. **stamped** : brought down heavily.

'The French army is ready to charge,' said the Earl of Salisbury, but a French messenger had arrived. 'Once more I come to ask you, King Henry, to surrender now before the battle begins.'

King Henry looked at the messenger. 'Tell your king that I and my troops will defeat your army or die.'

Before the battle, the English soldiers knelt and kissed the ground. Henry's army advanced and his archers fired their arrows into the French army. It was difficult for the French soldiers to move in their heavy armour through the mud and Henry's archers were very good. The French army were in trouble. By midday 8,000 French soldiers were dead, but only a few hundred English soldiers. When Montjoy came to Henry to ask if the French could bury their dead, Henry asked him if the English had won. Montjoy told him that they had.

When Henry saw Williams, the soldier he had exchanged gloves with the night before the battle, he called to him. 'Is this your glove?' Henry asked Williams.

Williams looked confused and surprised.

'It was me wearing an old brown cloak last night in the camp,' Henry said to Williams. 'You offended me when we met.'

'I didn't know you were my king,' said Williams. 'I thought you were an ordinary soldier. Please forgive me.'

Henry smiled. 'You fought well today. Fill Williams' glove with gold coins,' Henry said to the Duke of Exeter.

How happy everyone was when Henry crossed the English Channel. Men, women and boys were on the shore applauding and cheering. In London, everyone came out onto the streets to shout Henry's name. The Lord Mayor was dressed in his finest clothes. What a day of celebrations! Later Henry returned to France for an important meeting with the French king.

'Joy and good wishes to the King of France, the queen, and the beautiful Katharine,' said Henry. 'Good health to all you, lords of France.'

'We are happy to see you, King Henry,' said Charles. 'I hope today that we can make peace between England and France.'

'I hope so too,' said Henry. He intended to allow Charles to remain king, but there were some conditions. He wanted to marry Katharine. Everyone left the room to allow Henry and Katharine to be alone.

'Oh Katharine, any mistakes with your English do not matter if you can love me with your French heart. Maybe if your English were better, you might find me to be an ordinary king. Do you like me, Kate?' Henry asked.

'I do not understand. What is *like me*?'

Henry tried again. 'I'm just a soldier, not a poet. I cannot win your love with words. A poem is just a rhyme, but a man with a good heart is the sun and the moon. Take me for your husband and you will have a soldier. Take me for your husband and you will have a king. So, what do you say? Please speak, Katharine.'

'How can I love France's enemy?' said Katharine.

'I'm not France's enemy. Together we will rule England and France and have a son. I love you and I promise that the older I grow, the better I'll become. Old age cannot make my face worse than it already is! Take me by the hand and say "Harry of England, I'll marry you."'

Henry tried to kiss her hands and then her lips.

'It is not the custom of French girls to kiss before they marry,' said Katharine.

'We will make new customs,' said Henry and he kissed her on the lips.

When King Charles and his wife returned, they agreed to their daughter's marriage.

'Let's prepare for the wedding,' said Henry.

The text and **beyond**

1 Comprehension check
Answer the questions.

1 Why is Katharine learning English?
2 How did Henry react when he heard that Bardolph was caught for stealing?
3 Why were the French army confident?
4 What did Henry say to his soldiers on the night before the battle?
5 Why did Henry borrow an old brown cloak?
6 What challenge did Williams make to Henry?
7 On which feast day did the battle take place?
8 Did the French army win the battle of Agincourt?
9 How did the people of London celebrate this great victory?
10 Why did Katharine not want to kiss Henry?

2 Characters
Answer the questions with the name of one of the characters from the story.

Who...

1 surrendered his town to Henry?   ....
2 looked strong but was a coward?   ....
3 laughed at Henry's claim to the French throne?   ....
4 said Henry preferred banquets and sport when he was younger?   ....
5 offered Henry his beautiful daughter Katharine?   ....
6 gave passionate speeches?   ....
7 did not know that the man in the cloak was the king?   ....
8 did not speak good English?   ....

3 Henry's campaign in France
The sentences in this text are in the wrong order. Put them in the correct order and number them 1-8.

A ☐ The battle took place on 25th October 1415, St. Crispin's Day.
B ☐ After taking the city of Harfleur, Henry moved north to Calais.
C ☐ All the French leaders were killed or captured and the main battle lasted for half an hour.
D ☐ With a fleet of 300 ships, Henry set sail on 11th August 1415.
E ☐ The King of France agreed for his daughter Katharine to marry King Henry.
F ☐ The French army stopped Henry's march towards Calais, near the village of Agincourt. The English army was much smaller than the French army.
G ☐ The siege of Harfleur lasted for five weeks.
H ☐ They landed at Harfleur, in northern France.

49

 **FCE 4 Summary**

Read the summary of the story and decide which answer (A, B, C, or D) best fits each space. There is an example at the beginning (0).

The play is set in England in the 15th century. In his (**0**) ..*B*... Henry was a wild young man (**1**) .... met thieves (**2**) .... a tavern in London. When he becomes King of England, he (**3**) .... to change. Henry is convinced that he has a legal claim to (**4**) .... French throne and so he makes plans to attack France. The English army take the town of Harfleur and move on towards Calais. The two armies prepare for battle and even though the French army (**5**) .... five times larger than the English army, Henry wins. Henry returns (**6**) .... London in triumph before (**7**) .... peace with the French king. Henry marries Katharine and the marriage unites the two kingdoms.

0	**A**	young	**B**	youth	**C**	youths	**D**	younger
1	**A**	what	**B**	whose	**C**	which	**D**	who
2	**A**	at	**B**	to	**C**	by	**D**	from
3	**A**	must	**B**	have	**C**	should	**D**	has
4	**A**	the	**B**	/	**C**	a	**D**	an
5	**A**	are	**B**	was	**C**	is	**D**	were
6	**A**	in	**B**	to	**C**	from	**D**	/
7	**A**	makes	**B**	make	**C**	making	**D**	made

 INTERNET PROJECT

There are many film versions of *Henry V*. Connect to the Internet and find information about the one directed by Kenneth Branagh. Then answer the questions.

1 When was this film made?

2 Who provided the costumes for the film?

3 Which minor role was made larger for this film?

4 Who turned down the role of the King of France?

5 Who dubbed Kenneth Branagh for the French version of the film?

6 What happens to Bardolph in the film version which is different to the play?

Before you read

1 Look at the list of characters in the story before you start reading.

Flavius: a tribune — an official elected by the people
Murellus: a tribune
Cassius: a general and the head of the conspirators
Brutus: a supporter of the Republic and a conspirator
Mark Antony: a general and friend of Caesar
Julius Caesar: a great Roman general and senator
Cicero: a Roman senator
Decius: a conspirator
Portia: Brutus's wife
Calpurnia: Caesar's wife
Octavius: Caesar's nephew
Lepidus: the third member of Mark Antony and Octavius's coalition
Titinius: one of Cassius's friends

Setting: the city of Rome, in Italy, in 44 BCE.

2 **Listening**

Listen to the beginning of Part One. Caesar has just returned to Rome in triumph. You will hear the conversations of some people of Rome. For questions 1-8, complete the sentences.

After his victory Caesar wants to become **(1)** .... of Rome.
There are powerful and **(2)** .... forces conspiring against Caesar.
Many Romans are not working. They want to **(3)** .... Caesar's victory.
A fortune-teller tells Caesar to beware of **(4)** ....
Caesar thinks he is **(5)** ....
Brutus is **(6)** .... that Caesar will become King of Rome.
Cassius thinks that Brutus is more **(7)** .... than Caesar.
Caesar thinks that men like Cassius are **(8)** ....

3 **Vocabulary**
Complete the sentences with the correct words. The words are in Part One of *Julius Caesar.*

1   Someone who makes furniture from wood. ....
2   Something or someone that comes from another country. ....
3   Not right. ....
4   Inhabitants of a particular town or city. ....
5   When you do not take any notice of someone. ....

In the city of Rome in 44 BCE it was the feast of Lupercal ¹ in honour of the God Pan. For 450 years Rome had had a political system that did not allow one person to have all the power and rule as a king or emperor. But Julius Caesar had just returned to Rome in triumph after a victory in Spain over the sons of his old enemy Pompey the Great. He had become the most powerful man in the Roman Republic and wanted to become Emperor of Rome. But there were powerful and secret forces working against Caesar. Murellus and Flavius, two political enemies of Caesar, tried to stop people celebrating.

'Go home, you lazy men. Today isn't a holiday,' said Flavius to some men in the streets. 'What's your job?'

'I'm a carpenter,' said the man.

'Why aren't you in your shop today? Why are you leading these men through the streets?'

'We took the day off to see Caesar and celebrate his triumph,' said the man.

'You cruel men of Rome!' said Murellus. 'What's there to celebrate? You used to watch Pompey ride through the streets of Rome and cheer when you saw him. Caesar hasn't fought foreign enemies; he's fought a Roman so he can become a dictator!'

'Go home, you ungrateful men,' said Flavius. The men turned and left.

'What can we do? It's a feast day,' said Murellus.

1. **the feast of Lupercal** : the Roman feast of fertility held in the spring.

'Make sure that the statues are not decorated in honour of Caesar,' said Flavius. 'Caesar is becoming too powerful.'

A trumpet sounded and Caesar and his followers entered the square on their way to a celebration.

'Caesar!' called a fortune-teller in the crowd.

'Who's calling me?' said Caesar.

'Beware the Ides of March,' [2] came the voice of the fortune-teller.

'Bring this man to me,' Caesar said to Brutus. 'What did you say?'

'Beware the Ides of March,' said the fortune-teller. 'Something terrible will happen on March 15th.'

'He's insane,' said Caesar. 'Let's go.'

They left, but Cassius held Brutus's arm and asked him to stay and talk with him. 'I can tell that something's wrong. What's the matter Brutus?'

'I admire Caesar very much, but I'm afraid that he will become King of Rome. This would be good for him, but not for Rome,' said Brutus.

'You're right. Caesar stands like a Colossus over the world and we creep under his legs,' said Cassius. 'You are far more noble than Caesar, Brutus.'

'I'll think about what you have said,' replied Brutus.

When Caesar and his group returned, Caesar said to Mark Antony that he wanted the men around him to be healthy and happy. 'Look at Cassius over there. He thinks too much, and men like that are dangerous.'

'Don't worry about him, Caesar,' said Mark Antony.

'I prefer to avoid Cassius,' said Caesar before leaving the square.

'Casca,' Brutus said to one of Caesar's followers, 'Caesar's in a good mood. What happened today?'

'Mark Antony offered Caesar a crown three times, but each time Caesar refused it, the crowd expressed their love for him.'

Before Casca and Brutus left, Cassius agreed to meet them the next day to speak about the future of Rome. Cassius also decided to throw some notes through Brutus's window. The different handwriting seen on the various notes would show how many people were concerned about Caesar becoming Emperor of Rome. 'I want him to think that lots of citizens respect Brutus and are afraid of Caesar's ambition,' he said to himself.

---

2. **the Ides of March** : in the ancient Roman calendar, the 15th day of March, dedicated to the god Mars.

The weather had turned stormy. There was thunder and lightning when Casca met Cicero, a Roman senator, later that evening in a street in Rome.

'I've seen many storms,' said Casca, 'but never a storm that drops fire.'

'Is it an omen from the gods?' asked Cicero.

'First I saw a slave in the marketplace with his hand on fire. Then I met a lion near the Capitol. [3] The lion ignored me and walked past me. Then there was an owl hooting [4] at noon in the main square,' said Casca.

'Strange times,' said Cicero and he shook his head as he said goodnight to Casca.

When Cassius met Casca in the streets he had been wandering in the rain; he hadn't taken any shelter from the thunder and lightning.

'It's dangerous to go out in a storm,' said Casca. 'Why did you do it?'

'There is a man in Rome who is just like this dreadful night,' said Cassius. 'He thunders, throws lightning and roars [5] like the lion in the Capitol. This man is Caesar, and the storm is a warning from the gods because Caesar is threatening to destroy the Republic.'

'I'll join you if you plan to stop him,' said Casca.

'Casca, some of the most noble Romans are joining me in an honourable but dangerous mission,' Cassius said. 'You must help me to persuade Brutus to join us in this mission.'

'The people love Brutus,' said Casca.

'And that's why we need to get Brutus on our side before daylight,' replied Cassius.

It was night and Brutus was in his orchard walking and thinking. 'I haven't slept since my brother-in-law Cassius first began to tell me how powerful Caesar had become. Caesar will have to die,' muttered Brutus to himself. 'If Caesar is crowned king, it will change his character. It's a fact that power corrupts, so we must kill Caesar for the good of Rome.'

There was a knock at the door and Cassius and the group of conspirators entered. Brutus shook their hands.

'Let's swear an oath,' [6] said Cassius.

---

3. **Capitol** : the temple of Jupiter on the Capitoline Hill.
4. **hooting** : the sound an owl makes.
5. **roars** : makes a loud, deep sound.
6. **oath** : a solemn promise.

'No,' said Brutus, 'no oaths. Only weak people need to swear oaths.'

'Well, I think that Mark Antony should die with Caesar,' said Cassius.

'No,' said Brutus. 'That is too violent. Mark Antony won't cause us any problems once Caesar is dead. We must be bold [7] when we kill Caesar and we mustn't kill him in anger.'

'We don't know if Caesar will go to the Senate tomorrow,' said Cassius. 'The fortune-teller told him not to go out on the Ides of March.'

'If he is reluctant, I can convince him. I'll bring him to the Capitol,' said Decius.

'Brutus, friends, remember what you've said and remember that we do this for the good of Rome,' answered Cassius.

'Good morning to all of you,' said Brutus. The conspirators left and Portia, Brutus's wife, came into the garden. 'Brutus, my lord, what's the matter?'

'It's nothing. I'm not feeling well,' Brutus replied, but Portia knew that this was not true.

'I saw six or seven men hiding their faces, even though it was dark. But don't worry, I'll keep your secret.'

'I'll tell you later, my dear,' he said.

During this night of thunder and lightning, Calpurnia, Caesar's wife, had had a bad dream. 'Help! Someone please help! They're murdering Caesar,' she called out. In the morning she didn't want Caesar to leave the house.

'I will go out,' Caesar said. He pretended to be brave and told Calpurnia that he feared nothing and that he would die when it was necessary for him to die.

'The night watchman saw horrible things last night. Dead men were walking and ghosts were wandering through the city,' said Calpurnia.

Caesar smiled at his wife. 'The gods want to test my bravery. If I stayed at home today, I'd show everyone that I'm afraid. So I'll go out.'

'Please,' Calpurnia said, kneeling before him. 'Send Mark Antony to the Senate. He can tell them that you are unwell today.'

'Alright. To please you I'll stay at home,' replied Caesar.

Calpurnia was happy until Decius arrived. 'The Senate wanted to give you a crown today. If you don't go, they might change their minds. They might whisper that Caesar is afraid.'

On hearing this, Caesar felt foolish. 'Give me my robe. I'm going,' he said.

7. **bold** : brave.

The text and **beyond**

1 **Comprehension check**

For each question, mark the letter next to the correct answer — A, B, C or D.

1 In 44 BC Rome was

   A ☐ a monarchy.

   B ☐ a republic.

   C ☐ a dictatorship.

   D ☐ ruled by the Senate.

2 Some conspirators in Rome thought that

   A ☐ Caesar was becoming too powerful.

   B ☐ Rome should not be a republic.

   C ☐ Caesar should become emperor.

   D ☐ citizens should not vote.

3 A fortune-teller tells Caesar that 15th March

   A ☐ is his lucky day.

   B ☐ is the feast of Lupercal.

   C ☐ is the day he will become emperor.

   D ☐ is an unlucky day.

4 Cassius wants Brutus to think that

   A ☐ Caesar is his good friend.

   B ☐ the citizens want Caesar to be emperor.

   C ☐ the citizens are afraid of Caesar's ambition.

   D ☐ the citizens want Cassius to be emperor.

5 Brutus thinks that power

   A ☐ is good.

   B ☐ corrupts.

   C ☐ will strengthen Rome.

   D ☐ will improve Caesar's character.

6 Calpurnia

   A ☐ wants Caesar to go to the Senate.

   B ☐ wants Caesar to speak to the fortune-teller.

   C ☐ wants Caesar to test his bravery.

   D ☐ wants Caesar to stay at home.

If I stay at home today, I'll show everyone that I'm afraid.

The above sentence is a first conditional and it refers to a possible situation in the future. After the conjunction *if* we use a present tense with a future meaning. The second part of the sentence depends on the first.

If he doesn't stay at home, then he won't show everyone that he's afraid.

2 *If* **clauses**

Complete the sentences with the verbs in brackets in the correct form.

1 If Caesar .... emperor, the citizens of Rome will .... (become, suffer)
2 If Cassius .... Brutus, he'll .... the conspirators. (persuade, join)
3 'If you .... Caesar becoming emperor, I'll .... you,' said Casca. (stop, help)
4 If Caesar .... to the Senate, the conspirators will .... him. (go, kill)
5 'If Caesar .... reluctant, I'll .... him,' said Decius. (be, convince)

3 **Listening**

You will hear someone talking about the early life of Marcus Junius Brutus. Complete the notes (1-8) with the missing information.

> *Brutus was born in (1) .... BCE.*
> *His father was killed in (2) .... BCE.*
> *Brought up by Cato the (3) ....*
> *In Cyprus he received (4) .... interest from a loan.*
> *(5) .... was defeated.*
> *Brutus went on a mission to the (6) ....*
> *Caesar would not make Rome a (7) ....*
> *There were (8) .... conspirators.*

T: GRADE 7

4 **Speaking – National customs**

At the beginning of *Julius Caesar* they are celebrating the feast of Lupercal. Talk to a partner about national customs in your country. Ask and answer the questions.

1 Which national custom do you enjoy the most?
2 When is it and what do people do?
3 Do you wear special clothes?
4 Is there traditional food eaten at this time?
5 Does the custom involve decorating your house or village?
6 Why do you like it?

INTERNET PROJECT

Connect to the Internet and find information about Gaius Julius Caesar's life. Then answer the questions.

1 When was he born?
2 In which year did he hold a political position in Rome?
3 When did he become Governor of Gaul?
4 How did Pompey die?
5 What did Caesar do when he learned of Pomey's death?
6 When was Caesar named Dictator Perpetuus?

Now find information about the film *Julius Caesar* directed by Joseph L. Mankiewicz. Then answer the questions.

1 When was the film made?
2 Who starred as Julius Caesar?
3 Who played Brutus?
4 Who played Mark Antony?
5 Did the film receive any Oscar nominations?

Before you read

1 Prediction

What do you think will happen next in the story? Put a tick (✓) in the boxes.

1 ☐ Julius Caesar listens to a new warning and goes home.
2 ☐ The conspirators decide not to go through with their plan.
3 ☐ Brutus tells Caesar about the plan.
4 ☐ Caesar ignores all the warnings and goes to the Capitol.
5 ☐ The crowd persuades Caesar to turn back.

Read Part Two and check your ideas.

2 Reading pictures
Look at the picture on page 63 and answer the questions.

1 Which characters can we see in the picture?
2 What are the conspirators doing?
3 What can you see in the background?

3 Listening

FCE

Listen to the beginning of Part Two. You will hear about the assassination of Caesar. Choose the correct answer — A, B, C or D.

1 A man tried to give Caesar
   A ☐ a present.
   B ☐ a letter.
   C ☐ a knife.
   D ☐ a book.

2 Metellus asked Caesar to pardon his
   A ☐ mother.
   B ☐ son.
   C ☐ brother.
   D ☐ father.

3 Brutus says that death is
   A ☐ freedom.
   B ☐ a gift.
   C ☐ liberty.
   D ☐ peace.

4 When Mark Antony arrived the conspirators
   A ☐ welcomed him.
   B ☐ harmed him.
   C ☐ killed him.
   D ☐ punished him.

5 The crowd wanted
   A ☐ civil war.
   B ☐ a funeral.
   C ☐ a plan.
   D ☐ answers.

T

There were other people who wanted to warn Caesar about the Ides of
March. A man was standing on a street near the Capitol and waited for
Caesar to pass by on his way to the Senate. He had written a letter with all
the names of the conspirators. He hoped to give the letter to Caesar before
he reached the Senate. The fortune-teller was waiting on the road. He tried
once again to warn Caesar, but it was hopeless: Caesar ignored them both.

When Caesar entered the Capitol, Metellus ran up to him. The
conspirators had needed a reason to justify the assassination of Caesar and
Metellus had found one. 'Most mighty Caesar, you banished my brother.
Pardon him! Let him come home!' he said, but Caesar refused.

'Forgive him, Caesar,' said Brutus and Cassius, kneeling in front of him.

'Do you too want Metellus's brother to come back to Rome?' smiled
Caesar.

Decius too knelt on the steps. 'Great Caesar,' he said.

'Do you think you can convince me?' said Caesar.

'Hands speak for me!' said Casca as he stabbed Caesar. One by one all the
conspirators stabbed Caesar. As he fell, he looked at Brutus and said, '*Et tu,
Brute*?' [8] Then Caesar died.

---

8. **Et tu, Brute?** : You too, Brutus?

The crowd who were watching screamed.

'Death is a gift and we are Caesar's friends,' said Brutus. 'Let's wash our hands and swords in Caesar's blood and go to the Forum and shout "Peace, freedom and liberty!"'

Mark Antony's servant ran into the Senate. 'My master Mark Antony loved Caesar, but he will now serve Brutus if Brutus promises not to punish him.'

'Tell him he will not be harmed,' said Brutus.

The conspirators welcomed Mark Antony when he arrived.

'If you want to kill me too, then do it now. There's no better place to die than beside Caesar,' said Mark Antony.

'Don't ask us to kill you,' said Brutus. 'We seem cold and cruel but we did this because we love Rome and her people.'

'Let me speak at Caesar's funeral! That's all I ask,' said Mark Antony.

'Of course you can, Mark Antony,' said Brutus.

But Cassius was not happy about this. He was sure that Mark Antony would move the people against the conspirators. 'I don't like this plan,' he said.

When everyone had gone and Mark Antony was alone with the body, he said, 'Forgive me, Caesar, if I do not kill these murderers immediately. Italy will be ruined by civil war.'

Later Brutus and Cassius entered the Forum with a crowd.

'We want answers! Give us answers!' shouted the crowd.

Brutus climbed up onto the platform. 'You want to know the reasons why I killed Caesar? It's not because I didn't love him. It's because I loved Rome more. Caesar was great, but he was ambitious, and it's better that he is dead and that we can live as free men. Have I offended anyone?'

No one replied. After Brutus's speech the crowd believed that Caesar had been a tyrant and Brutus had been right to kill him. Then Mark Antony came in with Caesar's body. Before Brutus left he asked the crowd to listen to Mark Antony.

'Friends, Romans, countrymen, give me your attention,' he began. 'I have come here to bury Caesar, not to praise him. Brutus says that Caesar was ambitious and Brutus is an honourable man, but Caesar brought great wealth to Rome for the people. Was that ambition? When the poor cried, Caesar cried. You all loved him once,' and when Mark Antony stopped and cried, the crowd were sad. They remembered that Caesar had refused the crown and when Mark Antony brought out Caesar's will, [9] they asked him to read it.

'I can't read it,' said Mark Antony. 'It's not right for you to know how much Caesar loved you.'

'Read the will! We want to hear it, Mark Antony!' the crowd shouted.

'Make a circle around Caesar's body and I'll read it. You all know this cloak, don't you?' Mark Antony pointed to the stab wounds. 'Look! This was Cassius's dagger,' he said. 'Caesar loved Brutus and Brutus stabbed him. Caesar's blood ran down the steps of the Senate building.'

The crowd cried and became angry, and then Mark Antony read the will. Caesar had left money to every person in Rome. The crowd went wild and decided to burn the conspirators' houses. Brutus and Cassius had to run for their lives.

During this time of civil unrest, three men took control of Rome — Mark Antony, Octavius, Julius Caesar's nephew, and Lepidus. They made lists of people who had to be killed and they raised armies to fight Cassius and Brutus.

Brutus and Cassius met at a camp near Sardis, in western Turkey. Brutus criticised Cassius for taking bribes [10] and not paying his soldiers. 'We killed Caesar for justice,' he said. 'We cannot sell our honour for money.'

Brutus and Cassius quarrelled but finally they became friends again.

'Portia is dead,' said Brutus.

'How did she die?' asked Cassius.

'It was a terrible death! When she heard how strong Octavius and Mark Antony's armies were, she ate burning coal,' said Brutus.

'How horrible!' said Cassius.

'Octavius, Mark Antony and Lepidus have killed 100 senators,' said a soldier.

9. **will** : a document left by someone when they die leaving money and property.
10. **bribes** : money you give to somebody to persuade them to help you, especially by doing something dishonest.

'Well, we'll march to Philippi and meet Mark Antony's army tomorrow,' said Brutus.

They said goodnight, but while Brutus was reading in his tent, Caesar's ghost appeared.

'Tell me who you are!' said Brutus. 'Are you a god, an angel or a devil?'

'I'm your evil spirit,' said the ghost.

'Why are you here?' asked Brutus.

'I'm here to tell you that you will see me at the battle.'

'See you at Philippi?' said Brutus. The ghost disappeared and when Brutus asked the other men if they had seen anything, they said no.

Cassius was afraid that the battle would not go well. He knew that he and Brutus would never walk in chains through the streets of Rome. The battle did not go well for Cassius's army. Mark Antony's army defeated them, but when he heard that Brutus's army was fighting well against Octavius, he sent his best friend Titinius to get more news. As Cassius watched, he thought he saw his friend captured.

'What have I done?' he cried. 'I'm such a coward to send my best friend to his death.' It was too much for Cassius and he ordered his servant to kill him with his own sword.

'Brutus is winning! This news will comfort Cassius!' Titinius said. He had not been captured and when he returned with news of the battle he found Cassius's body. Titinius cried for the terrible mistake and in his sorrow stabbed himself and died.

Brutus was sad when he heard of Cassius's death. 'I'll try to find time to cry for you, Cassius, but now we'll try our luck in a second battle.'

The armies fought again, but this time Brutus lost.

'The ghost of Caesar came to me on the battlefield and told me that the time had come for me to die,' Brutus said to his men. 'I must die an honourable death. Hold my sword for me!' Then he run on it.

When Mark Antony found Brutus's body, he said, 'This man was the noblest Roman of them all. The other conspirators were jealous of Caesar, but Brutus was honest. He was a rare example of a real man.'

The text and **beyond**

FCE ① Comprehension check

For each question, mark the letter next to the correct answer — A, B, C or D.

1 Caesar ignored
   A ☐ the warnings.
   B ☐ the conspirators.
   C ☐ Metellus's brother.
   D ☐ Cassius's brother.

2 Mark Antony asks
   A ☐ to speak to the conspirators.
   B ☐ to speak to Calpurnia.
   C ☐ to speak at Caesar's funeral.
   D ☐ to speak to Cassius.

3 Brutus says he killed Caesar
   A ☐ because he loved him.
   B ☐ because he didn't love him.
   C ☐ because he wasn't ambitious.
   D ☐ because he loved Rome.

4 Mark Antony tells the crowd that Caesar
   A ☐ was ambitious.
   B ☐ loved the people.
   C ☐ took the crown.
   D ☐ was honourable.

5 Three men took control of Rome. They were
   A ☐ Brutus, Cassius and Lepidus.
   B ☐ Mark Antony, Casca and Brutus.
   C ☐ Octavius, Mark Antony and Lepidus.
   D ☐ Octavius, Lepidus and Cassius.

6 Cassius and Brutus
   A ☐ die in battle.
   B ☐ are killed by a ghost.
   C ☐ stab each other.
   D ☐ die an honourable death.

2 Vocabulary

Complete the summary of Parts One and Two of *Julius Caesar*. Choose words from the list. There are some extra words that you don't need.

> won   noblest   horrible   person   find   triumph
> raise   crowd   strong   ignores   defeated   honourable
> convinces   praise   assassinate   dream   persuade   powerful

At the beginning of the play Julius Caesar has **(1)** .... the sons of Pompey and returns to Rome in **(2)** .... A fortune-teller tells Caesar that he will die on 15th March but Caesar **(3)** .... him. There are fears that Caesar is becoming too **(4)** .... Cassius persuades Brutus to join a group of conspirators and **(5)** .... Caesar and although Brutus agrees, he **(6)** .... them not to kill Mark Antony.

Calpurnia has a terrible **(7)** .... She fears for Caesar's life and she tries to **(8)** .... him not to go to the Senate. He goes and the conspirators kill him. Brutus gains support from the citizens of Rome when he explains why they killed Caesar, but it is Mark Antony's words that make the **(9)** .... feel anger for Caesar's death. The mob turn on the conspirators and Cassius and Brutus run away.

Mark Antony, Lepidus and Octavius **(10)** .... an army and meet Cassius and Brutus in battle. Brutus and Cassius prefer to die **(11)** .... deaths than be captured. Mark Antony pays tribute to Brutus saying that he was the **(12)** .... Roman of them all.

3 Characters

Match a character (A-G) to a sentence (1-10) that describes him/her. The people may be chosen more than once.

A   Caesar

B   Mark Antony

C   Brutus

D   Casca

E   Cassius

F   Calpurnia

G   Caesar's ghost

1   ☐ is afraid that Caesar will become King of Rome.

2   ☐ has become the most powerful man in Rome.

3   ☐ throws notes through Brutus's window.

4   ☐ sees a slave with his hand on fire.

5   ☐ refuses the crown three times.

6   ☐ thinks Mark Antony should die with Caesar.

7   ☐ tells Caesar to send Mark Antony to the Senate.

8   ☐ says Caesar was great, but he was ambitious.

9   ☐ says that Brutus is an honourable man.

10   ☐ says 'I'm your evil spirit.'

 **4** Read the text below and think of the word which best fits each space. Use only one word in each space. There is an example at the beginning (**0**).

The Government in Roman Times

Before Julius Caesar took control in 48 BCE Rome was a republic and it
(**0**) ....was........................ ruled by two consuls, who were elected
(**1**) .... the citizens of Rome. The Romans were divided
(**2**) .... different classes. The Patricians were
(**3**) .... wealthy citizens of Rome (**4**) ....
lived in large houses with slaves working for them. Men were allowed to go to the
Assembly (**5**) .... vote, but women and slaves could not.

Plebians were the working classes. Many of (**6**) .... were
tradesmen or craftsmen and they were allowed to vote. When there were
elections, the citizens voted for two consuls, (**7**) .... served
for one year. The consuls governed Rome and they both had to agree on all
decisions. Tribunes were also elected by the people and their job was to
(**8**) .... sure that citizens were treated fairly. The Senate
(**9**) .... advice to the two consuls and it was the centre of
administration for the Roman government. Senators were retired magistrates
and they knew a lot (**10**) .... government. There were about
600 men in the Senate and they usually came (**11**) .... rich
noble families. However, the Senate could (**12**) .... always
control the Roman army and generals sometimes fought
(**13**) .... another. While the Senate existed Rome was the
greatest power in the Mediterranean and in Europe.

The Three Witches by J. H. Fussli (1783).

The Dark Side of Shakespeare's Plays:
Revenge, Ghosts and Witches

Revenge tragedies

'Revenge his foul and most unnatural murder.' Hamlet *Act, 1 scene V.*

Medieval and Renaissance England were vengeful eras. Blood feuds were settled by a duel or other violent action. Private acts of revenge were justified if a wrong had been committed to a person or their family. Francis Bacon, a senior lawyer in the court of Queen Elizabeth, described revenge actions as 'a sort of wild justice' and the state under Queen Elizabeth I was keen to take control of the justice system. The Tudors wanted to replace blood feuds with a legal system and with bureaucracy, and eliminate the medieval code of private revenge, which had become a way of life for many people.

All revenge tragedy came from the Greeks, who wrote and performed the first organised plays. Later, it was the Roman playwright Seneca (ca. 4 BCE – 65 CE) who laid down the rules for revenge tragedies that were to become so popular in the Renaissance period. Some of the Senecan devices which can also be observed in Elizabethan tragedies are the following: five act structure, the appearance of a ghost, and long rhetorical speeches.

Ghosts

In Elizabethan England people were superstitious and they believed that ghosts existed and penetrated daily life. They told ghost stories by the firelight in many households. Ghosts were also a popular theatrical device, and they often appeared

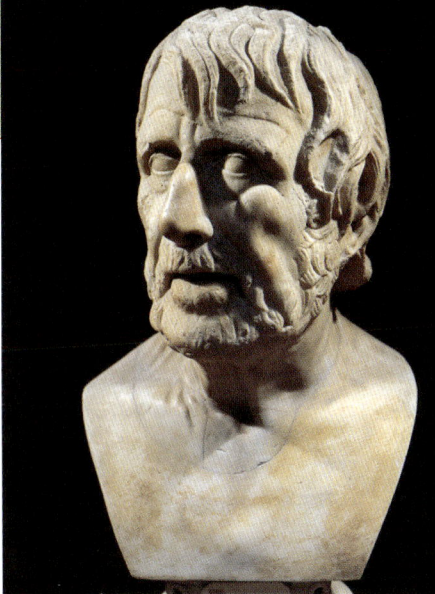

Portrait of Seneca.

on stage. Shakespeare often used ghosts to persuade their victims to take revenge on someone or to remember someone. There is a good example of this in *Hamlet*, where the ghost of King Hamlet calls for revenge.

We can distinguish two types of ghosts in Shakespeare's plays: the subjective or vision ghost is only visible to the person with whom it is directly connected. For example, Macbeth is the only one who sees the ghost of Banquo, and Richard III is troubled in his sleep by the spirits of those that he killed. On the other hand, the objective ghost, like Old Hamlet, presents itself to several people. Although Shakespeare took ghosts in his plays seriously, we cannot be sure if he believed in them. He used ghosts to reflect on our world, even if we can never be certain what they were trying to tell us.

Witches

Women did not have any rights in Elizabethan society, with the exception of the Queen. They were expected to be obedient firstly to their fathers and then to their husbands. They could not go to university and only noble women were given a good education. Women could not become lawyers, doctors or politicians and they could not act on the stage. Women worked in the house while men travelled. There were 'wise women' in England, who lived in the countryside. They were medical professionals of their time with a great knowledge of plants and herbs. Some used herbs like mandrake [1] and hemlock [2] and they passed on their

1. **mandrake** : a southern European plant. The root looks like the human body.
2. **hemlock** : a poisonous plant.

knowledge to their daughters. By the time Elizabeth came to the throne, these wise women were seen as witches and Elizabethans considered witchcraft to be devil worship. Single women and old women were often accused of practising witchcraft. The Catholic Church classed any woman with knowledge of herbs as a witch and even though monasteries had herb gardens and monks knew a lot about the power of herbs, they were never looked upon suspiciously.

Elizabethans and Jacobeans blamed unexplained events such as deaths, bad harvests and fires as the work of witches. During the Elizabethan and Jacobean ages there were 270 witch trials.

One of the best examples of the representation of witches can be found in *Macbeth*. In Macbeth, the weird sisters or witches represent the dark side of the human psyche and man's constant struggle against the powers of evil. They tempt Macbeth and unlike Banquo, Macbeth is not able to think rationally. Time passes and Macbeth is influenced more and more by the witches. They put ideas into his head and the dark side of his character becomes twisted.

1 Comprehension check

Look at each statements. Is it correct or incorrect? If it is correct tick the box under A for YES. If you think it isn't correct tick the box under B for NO.

		A	B
1	During Shakespeare's time, family disputes were rarely settled by private acts of revenge.	☐	☐
2	Queen Elizabeth I was not keen on having a justice system.	☐	☐
3	The Greeks invented revenge tragedies.	☐	☐
4	All Shakespeare's ghosts appear to incite revenge.	☐	☐
5	All women in Elizabethan England could attend university.	☐	☐
6	Women who used herbs to cure people of illness were called witches.	☐	☐
7	There were only a few witch trials during the Elizabethan and Jacobean ages.	☐	☐

Before you read

1 Look at the list of characters in the story before you start reading.

Hamlet: Prince of Denmark
Claudius: King of Denmark, Hamlet's uncle
Gertrude: Queen of Denmark, Hamlet's mother
Polonius: the Lord Chamberlain
Horatio: Hamlet's close friend
Ophelia: Polonius's daughter
Laertes: Polonius's son
Fortinbras: Prince of Norway
the ghost of Hamlet's father
Rosencrantz: a courtier and friend of Hamlet from university
Guildenstern: a courtier and friend of Hamlet from university
Marcellus: an officer
Bernardo: an officer
Francisco: a soldier

Setting: Denmark in the Middle Ages.

2 Reading

Read the beginning of Part One. Choose the most suitable heading for each part (A-D). There is one extra heading which you do not need to use.

1 ☐ A snake in the grass
2 ☐ A happy prince
3 ☐ Murder most foul
4 ☐ An evil king
5 ☐ A ghostly experience

3 Vocabulary

Match a word in A with a definition in B. Use your dictionary if necessary.

A			B	
1	☐	grief	A	to call someone with your head or hand
2	☐	shame	B	to feel compassion for someone
3	☐	mist	C	extreme sadness, usually when someone dies
4	☐	wedding	D	a painful feeling over something dishonourable
5	☐	beckon	E	a marriage ceremony
6	☐	pity	F	a light fog

Everything was not well in the country of Denmark. The king was dead and  Gertrude, his queen, had married her husband's brother, Claudius. Some people suspected that Claudius had killed his brother so that he could marry Gertrude and become King of Denmark.

Prince Hamlet had returned from his studies in Wittenberg to attend his father's funeral and, after that, his mother's wedding to his uncle Claudius. Prince Hamlet was troubled. He felt grief for his father's death and shame for his mother's marriage. How could his mother have forgotten his father so quickly? He had been a loving and gentle husband to her.

Strange things were happening at the Castle of Elsinore. Even the guards were afraid as they looked into the night sky. It was nearly midnight and Francisco, a night watchman, was standing in the cold mist on the gun platform [1] of Elsinore Castle. Footsteps echoed on the stone floor.

'Who's there?' Francisco's voice was high and frightened.

'Long live the king,' came a voice through the mist. It was Bernardo, who had arrived to take Francisco's place.

---

1. **gun platform** : the flat high part of the castle where the cannons are.

As Francisco was leaving, Marcellus, another watchman, and Horatio, a friend of Prince Hamlet, arrived. Bernardo and Marcellus wanted to show Horatio something. For the past few nights a ghost had appeared to them. It looked like the ghost of old King Hamlet, who had recently died. Horatio did not believe they had seen a ghost.

'It's just your imagination. There is no ghost,' he said.

Just as Horatio spoke these words, the clock struck midnight and the ghost came. It was pale, with a dark silvery beard, and it walked with great sadness.

'I order you to speak,' said Horatio, but the ghost did not answer. Horatio and Bernardo followed the ghost as it walked slowly around the gun platform. Once it lifted its head and was about to speak, but at that moment morning came, and it vanished.

Horatio trembled and looked pale. The ghost wore armour — this was a bad omen. Prince Fortinbras, the nephew of the King of Norway, wanted to invade Denmark and Horatio felt that the ghost was warning them of danger.

'Quick, we must find young Hamlet. The ghost didn't want to speak to me, but it will speak to its only son.'

In the Great Hall of Elsinore Castle, the court was assembled and Claudius spoke solemnly. 'I can never forget my brother Hamlet, but life must go on. Young Fortinbras is a threat and my nephew and my son Prince Hamlet is always so sad. You must understand, Hamlet, that all fathers die. All sons must lose their fathers,' Claudius said to Hamlet.

'I wear black clothes, but I have more grief inside than you can see on my face,' replied Hamlet.

It was only once Claudius and his court had left, that Hamlet could speak his true thoughts aloud in the empty Great Hall.

'My mother's marriage to Claudius disgusts me and I am not sure how my father died. Claudius said that a snake bit him, but I suspect the snake to be my uncle Claudius. I am sure that the snake that killed my father now wears the crown!'

These thoughts filled his mind.

'What should I think of my mother's part in this? Did she know of the murder? Did she even agree to it?' This growing suspicion that his mother knew of the murder or had even agreed to it, was driving Hamlet mad.

'Why are women so weak?' he cried out. 'This incestuous marriage can only lead to disaster.'

When Horatio, Bernardo and Marcellus arrived to tell him their story, Hamlet listened. From their description of the ghost with the dark silvery beard, the young prince believed that they had seen his father's ghost.

'I'll watch with you tonight. Maybe the ghost will come again,' he said to Horatio.

'I think it will,' replied Horatio.

'If it looks like my father, I'll speak to it. See you on the gun platform between eleven and twelve,' Hamlet said.

When night came Hamlet took his place with Horatio and Marcellus. In the darkness Horatio was the first to see the ghost moving towards them.

'Look, my lord, it is coming.'

'May the angels protect us,' Hamlet muttered, 'because I don't know if you are a good or an evil spirit. I will speak to you and call you Hamlet, King, Father, Royal Dane!'

The ghost beckoned to him. It wanted young Hamlet to follow him to a quiet place. Horatio and Marcellus tried to stop the prince from following the ghost. In its silvery armour it looked so pale and terrifying that they were afraid it was an evil spirit sent to harm the prince. But Hamlet decided to follow him.

'Dawn approaches,' said the ghost 'and I must return to purgatory.'

Its body shook as it gave the deepest sigh.

'Oh, poor ghost,' whispered Hamlet.

'Don't pity me, but listen to what I must tell you,' said the ghost, as it drew Hamlet further away from where anyone might overhear their conversation.

When it was sure that they were quite alone, the spirit told Hamlet that it was the ghost of his father, the king. He had been murdered by his own brother, Claudius, who wanted his wife and the crown of Denmark. It had happened as he was asleep in the garden one afternoon. His brother had come silently into the orchard and poured poison in his ear.

'Revenge! I want revenge for the terrible murder,' the ghost said.

'Claudius has poisoned Denmark and corrupted Gertrude, my wife, but I want you to leave your mother's punishment to God. Goodbye, Hamlet. Remember me,' the ghost said, and then it vanished.

Hamlet returned to the others. He was agitated, and afraid that Claudius might suspect that he knew more about his father's death. He decided to pretend to be mad. Hamlet's clothes, speech and behaviour became wild. The king and queen were concerned. They thought that the cause of this must be love. Hamlet loved a beautiful girl called Ophelia, the daughter of Polonius, the king's chief minister. He sent her letters and rings and had told her how much he loved her. Hamlet had not seen Ophelia much since his father's death and Polonius had told his daughter to forget Hamlet. Claudius and Gertrude were sure that love was the cause of Hamlet's madness.

So that he could find out more, Claudius had asked two of Hamlet's friends to come to the castle.

'Welcome, dear Rosencrantz and Guildenstern,' said Claudius. 'I sent for [2] you because I need your help. Hamlet has changed and I would like you to stay here and discover what's wrong.'

'I hope we can make Hamlet happy,' said Guildenstern, and they went to look for Hamlet.

'What are you doing here at Elsinore?' Hamlet asked them when they met.

'Visiting you, my lord,' said Rosencrantz.

'Come on, tell me the truth,' replied Hamlet.

'The king asked us to come,' said Guildenstern.

Doubt about the ghost had been growing in Hamlet's mind. 'I need more evidence,' he thought. 'The ghost I have seen may be an evil spirit.' It was at that moment that a group of travelling actors arrived and a plan came into his head. Hamlet asked the actors to stage *The Murder of Gonzago* the following night and include an extra speech. The plot was like the murder of King Hamlet. The play told the story of Lucianus, a relation of Duke Gonzago, who poisoned him in his garden and won the love of Duke Gonzago's wife. If Claudius was the murderer, then his guilt would show on his face as he watched the play.

'With this play,' he thought, 'I'll see if Claudius is the murderer.'

The next day Rosencrantz and Guildenstern visited the king and queen.

2. **sent for** : ordered (you) to come.

'We don't understand why Hamlet is sad, but he is looking forward to the play.' Encouraged, Gertrude and Claudius agreed to see the play that evening.

Claudius wanted to see Ophelia and Hamlet together, so he and Polonius hid where they knew they would meet. They were not disappointed because when Hamlet entered he was talking to himself.

'To be or not to be, that is the question,' Hamlet wondered. 'Is it better to live or die? Life is miserable, but because we do not know what will come in the afterlife, we have to live. I would like to die, if death were like a dreamless sleep...To die, to sleep... Maybe to dream. That's the problem. For in that sleep of death, what dreams may come when we have left this mortal world.'

His thoughts were interrupted by Ophelia. Controlled by her interfering father, Polonius, she had been sent to return Hamlet's letters and gifts. Hamlet was angry with all women. He saw them as weak, frail and untrustworthy, because his mother had forgotten his father so quickly and married his uncle.

'Go and live in a nunnery,' [3] he told her. 'It is better to do that than bring children into this world. It would have been better if my mother had not given birth to me.'

'He is mad,' Ophelia said once Hamlet had gone.

Claudius was alarmed at what he had heard. He realised that his nephew was a threat and decided to send him to England with Rosencrantz and Guildenstern to collect some money he was owed.

'After the play, let Gertrude speak to Hamlet,' Polonius suggested. 'She will discover what is wrong with her son.'

That evening, Hamlet anxiously showed the players how to act the parts he had written for them. Hamlet sat close to Claudius to watch his expression. The play began and Claudius's face became white. When the murderer, Lucianus, poured poison in Gonzago's ear, Claudius stood up.

'Light! Bring torches!' Claudius called to the servants. 'I feel ill,' he said, and hurried from the theatre. The play was stopped, but Hamlet had seen enough. The words of the ghost were true.

---

3. **nunnery** : convent.

The text and **beyond**

1 Comprehension check
Answer the questions.

1 How did Hamlet feel about his mother's marriage to his uncle?
2 What had Bernardo and Marcellus seen over the past few nights on the castle ramparts?
3 Why did Horatio think it was a bad omen to see a ghost wearing armour?
4 What suspicions did Hamlet have over his father's death?
5 Where did the ghost have to return to at dawn?
6 How was the old king murdered?
7 Why did Claudius send for Rosencrantz and Guildenstern?
8 Why did Hamlet want the actors to perform *The Murder of Gonzago*?
9 How did Hamlet realise that the ghost's words were true?

2 Vocabulary
Find the word that does not belong with the other three words and then explain why. All the words come from Part One of the story.

1 ghost/apparition/madness/spirit
2 crept/footsteps/followed/walked
3 kill/murder/assassinate/murderer

4 whispered/beckoned/muttered/replied
5 servants/actors/theatre/play
6 disorder/alarmed/afraid/troubled

3 Fill in the gaps with one of the six 'odd words out' in exercise 2.

1 When the murderer Lucianus poured poison in Gonzago's ear, Claudius stood up and called for the .... to bring light.
2 .... echoed on the stone floor.
3 Claudius and Gertrude were sure that love was the cause of Hamlet's ....
4 If Claudius were the ...., then his guilt would show on his face as he watched the play.
5 The ghost .... to him.
6 There was .... in the country of Denmark.

4 Characters
Answer the questions with the name of a character from the story.

Who...
1 sees the ghost first? ....
2 has married quickly after her husband's death? ....
3 thinks that the ghost is in the guards' imagination? ....
4 has more grief inside than on his face? ....
5 wants to leave Gertrude's punishment to heaven? ....
6 is controlled by her father? ....

Claudius said that a snake had bitten King Hamlet.

We use the past perfect:

- to refer to a time earlier than another past time. By using the past perfect, we make the order of events clear.

  His brother had crept silently into the orchard and poured poison in his ear.

Be careful! When we use *before* and *after* the sequence of events are clear and we do not use the past perfect.

After he went into the orchard, he poured poison in the king's ear.

- in reported speech.

  The ghost told Hamlet that he had been murdered by his brother Claudius.

5 **Past simple and past perfect**

Complete the sentences with the past simple or the past perfect of the verbs.

1 King Hamlet .... (die) while Hamlet his son .... (be) at university.

2 Young Hamlet .... (suspect) that his father .... (be) murdered.

3 When Hamlet .... (speak) to Horatio, Horatio .... (see) the ghost of the old king.

4 Claudius .... (enter) the orchard and .... (pour) poison in his ear.

5 When Hamlet .... (come) into the room, he did not know that Claudius and Polonius .... (hide) behind a curtain.

6 Ophelia .... (say) Hamlet was mad, once Hamlet .... (go).

6 **Put the following sentences into the correct chronological order.**

A ☐ Claudius asks Rosencrantz and Guildenstern to spy on Hamlet.

B ☐ Hamlet is angry with all women and tells Ophelia to go and live in a nunnery.

C ☐ When Hamlet comes home for his father's funeral, he finds that his mother has married his uncle.

D ☐ During the play Claudius becomes pale and Hamlet knows he is guilty.

E ☐ Hamlet pretends to be mad.

F ☐ An apparition, which looks like the old king, appears to the guards.

G ☐ Claudius says that a snake killed Hamlet's father, but Hamlet suspects that the snake is Claudius.

H ☐ Hamlet asks some travelling actors to put on the play *The Murder of Gonzago*.

I ☐ The ghost of Hamlet's father tells him that he was murdered by his own brother.

J ☐ Horatio takes Hamlet to see the ghost.

Before you read

FCE

8 **1** **Listening**

Listen to the beginning of Part Two. You will hear a conversation between Hamlet and his mother Gertrude. Choose the correct answer — A, B, C or D.

1 Claudius is in a room
  A ☐ praying for forgiveness.
  B ☐ planning revenge.
  C ☐ claiming his reward.
  D ☐ getting his crown.

2 Who is hiding in Gertrude's chamber?
  A ☐ Claudius
  B ☐ Hamlet
  C ☐ Polonius
  D ☐ Ophelia

3 Gertrude is
  A ☐ her brother's wife's husband.
  B ☐ her husband's father's wife.
  C ☐ her husband's brother's wife.
  D ☐ her husband's son's wife.

4 Hamlet kills
  A ☐ Gertrude.
  B ☐ Polonius.
  C ☐ Claudius.
  D ☐ Ophelia.

5 Hamlet thinks that
  A ☐ Gertrude didn't know about the plan to kill her husband.
  B ☐ Gertrude did know about the plan to kill her husband.
  C ☐ Gertrude killed her husband.
  D ☐ Gertrude was forced to kill her husband.

6 When the ghost arrives
  A ☐ Gertrude thinks she is going mad.
  B ☐ Gertrude is afraid.
  C ☐ Gertrude can see the ghost.
  D ☐ Gertrude can't see the ghost.

2 **Prediction**

Answer the questions. Discuss your ideas with a partner.

1 Is Hamlet going mad or is it just an act?
2 Will Hamlet avenge his father's death?
3 Will Hamlet forgive his mother and marry Ophelia?

In a panic, Claudius ran to a room in the castle where he fell onto his knees **and prayed.**

'Forgive me my horrible murder,' he asked, but he knew that prayer wouldn't work. He still had the rewards of his murder... his crown and his queen.

'So what can I do? I can only ask the angels for help,' Claudius whispered.

Gertrude had asked to speak to Hamlet in her room. On his way Hamlet saw Claudius praying, but before he could decide what form his revenge should take, he had to speak to his mother.

In Gertrude's room Polonius had hidden behind a tapestry. [4]

'Why have you sent for me?' Hamlet said when he rushed into the room.

'You have offended your father!' Gertrude said.

'Mother, you have offended *my* father.'

'Do not forget who you are speaking to,' said the queen.

'Oh, I wish I could forget. You are now the wife of your husband's brother and you are my mother, though I wish you weren't.'

Hamlet took her by the wrists and made her sit down. Gertrude was frightened and she cried out.

'Help! Help the queen!' came a voice from behind the tapestry.

4. **tapestry** : a picture made of cloth, which hangs on a wall.

'Claudius,' muttered Hamlet. He drew his sword and thrust it into the tapestry.

There was a cry. When Hamlet pulled the body out, it was not Claudius, but Polonius, the king's minister. He had been spying on them.

'Goodbye, you intruding fool,' said Hamlet.

'What have you done?' screamed Gertrude.

'A terrible act, Mother, but not as bad as yours when you killed your husband and married his brother,' replied Hamlet. He showed her a picture of the dead king and a picture of Claudius. 'What nobility there is in my father's face,' he told her. 'Look how ugly Claudius is, a man who killed his own brother.'

It was as he was speaking to his mother that the ghost of his father entered the room. Hamlet was afraid, but he asked the ghost why it was there.

'To remind you of the revenge you promised me.'

The ghost told Hamlet to speak to his mother before fear and grief killed her. Then it disappeared.

Gertrude could not see the ghost. 'My son is mad,' she said.

'I'm not mad,' said Hamlet. 'Your sins have brought my father's spirit to earth again. Keep away from Claudius,' and Hamlet left, dragging the body of Polonius with him.

The death of Polonius gave Claudius the excuse to send Hamlet to England, and he sent him on a ship with Rosencrantz and Guildenstern. Suspecting a trap, Hamlet found a letter written by Claudius. The letter said that Prince Hamlet should be put to death as soon as he arrived in England. Hamlet rubbed out his name and wrote the names of Rosencrantz and Guildenstern on the letter.

The ship sailed through a dangerous part of the ocean and when a pirate ship attacked, Hamlet jumped bravely onto the deck. Hamlet's ship sailed away with Rosencrantz and Guildenstern continuing their journey to England without him. The pirates were kind and when they discovered that Hamlet was a prince, they took him back to Denmark. Hamlet sent a message to Elsinore saying that he would return the next day.

There was tragic news when Hamlet returned. The first thing he saw was the funeral of Ophelia. She had begun to lose her mind the day her father, Polonius, was killed by the man she loved. One day Ophelia had taken flowers to hang in a tree. The branch had broken and she had fallen into a stream and drowned.

Laertes, Polonius's son, had returned from France. He wanted to avenge his father's death and now his sister's, too. It was only when Hamlet saw Ophelia in her grave that he knew how much he loved her.

'I loved her more than 30,000 brothers,' Hamlet said to Laertes. He begged Laertes to forgive him and for a time they were friends.

However, Claudius wanted Laertes to kill Hamlet. He persuaded Laertes to challenge Hamlet to a friendly sword fight. Both swords should have been blunt, 5 but Claudius dipped Laertes's sword in poison. Claudius also prepared a goblet 6 of poisoned wine for Hamlet when he became thirsty.

At first Laertes fought gently. He allowed Hamlet to gain some advantage. Claudius pretended to be pleased and praised Hamlet's success. But soon Laertes cut Hamlet with his poisoned sword. Hamlet became more violent and in the struggle both swords fell to the ground. When they picked them up, Hamlet had Laertes's poisoned sword. With one thrust he stabbed him. Laertes fell and at that moment Gertrude cried out.

'The drink! The drink!' she screamed. She had drunk from the poisoned goblet that her husband had prepared for Hamlet.

Gertrude was dead and Hamlet knew that he did not have long to live. It was time to avenge his father's murder.

Hamlet turned on his false uncle. He pushed the poisoned sword into Claudius's heart, then forced him to drink the rest of the poisoned wine.

Hamlet's breath was faint. 'Horatio, tell everyone what happened. Fortinbras, you will be the next King of Denmark...'

Fortinbras ordered Hamlet's body to be carried away like a soldier and Horatio cried and promised he would tell the world the remarkable story of his dear friend Hamlet, Prince of Denmark.

---

5. **blunt** : a knife or sword not having a sharp edge or point.
6. **goblet** : a glass or cup for wine.

6 Revenge

Below are some quotes about revenge. Read them with your partner and choose the four that you like best. Then vote as a class on the two best quotes.

An eye for an eye makes the whole world blind.

Mahatma Ghandi (political leader of India, 1869-1948)

Something of vengeance I had tasted for the first time; as aromatic wine it seemed, on swallowing warm and racy: it's after flavour metallic and corroding, gave me a sensation as if I had been poisoned.

Charlotte Brontë (English novelist, 1816-1855)

Revenge… is like a rolling stone, which, when a man hath forced up a hill, will return upon him with a greater violence, and break those bones whose sinews gave it motion.

Albert Schweitzer (medical missionary, 1875-1965)

Tis more noble to forgive, and more manly to despise, than to revenge an injury.

Benjamin Franklin
(American scientist, inventor and statesman, 1706-1790)

The best revenge is massive success.

Frank Sinatra (American singer and actor, 1915-1998)

It is impossible to suffer without making someone pay for it; every complaint already contains revenge.

Friedrich Nietzsche (German philosopher, 1844-1900)

The best revenge is to be unlike him who performed the injury.

Marcus Aurelius (Roman Emperor, 121-180)

Sweet is revenge — especially to women.

Lord Byron (English poet, 1788-1824)

When a man steals your wife there is no better revenge than to let him keep her.

Sacha Guitry (French director and playwright, 1885-1957)

Now in pairs try and write your own definition. Compare your answers as a class.

....

....

FCE ⑦ Sentence transformation

Complete the second sentence so that it has a similar meaning to the first sentence, using the word given. Do not change the word given. You must use between two and five words, including the word given. Here is an example (0).

0 The ghost resembled old King Hamlet.

LIKE   The ghost ...looked like........................... old King Hamlet.

1 Some people suspected that Claudius had killed his brother.

OF   Claudius .... his brother by some people.

2 'I'll watch with you tonight.'

THAT   Hamlet said .... with his friends that night.

3 The ghost was either good or evil.

IF   Hamlet didn't .... good or evil.

4 Suspicion was growing in Hamlet's mind.

MORE   Hamlet .... suspicious.

5 Hamlet was starting to find Polonius irritating.

NERVES   Polonius was getting ....

⑧ Speaking

Look at these two photographs. Compare and contrast them and then say which you think would make the most interesting setting for a book or film and why. With your partner choose one of the photos and plan your story. Use the prompts to help you. Then tell your story to the class.

- Decide who lives in the castle.
- Decide when your story is set.
- Something terrible has happened in the castle. What?
- Someone comes to solve the crime. Who? What are they like?
- Decide on a suitable conclusion to your story.

Before you read

1 Look at the list of characters in the story before you start reading.

Duncan: King of Scotland
Macbeth: Thane of Glamis and friend of King Duncan
Lady Macbeth: Macbeth's wife
Banquo: a Scottish general
Malcolm: Duncan's eldest son
Donalbain: Duncan's younger son
Macduff: Thane of Fife
Fleance: Banquo's son
Ross: Thane of Scotland
Three witches
A doctor

Setting: Scotland in the 11th century.

2 Listening

Listen to the beginning of Part One. You will hear a conversation between Macbeth, Banquo and three hideous witches. Decide if each sentence is correct or incorrect. If it is correct put a tick (✓) in the box under A for YES. If it is not correct put a tick (✓) in the box under B for NO.

		A	B
1	The weather is fine when Macbeth and Banquo meet the witches.	☐	☐
2	Banquo asks the witches if they are ghosts.	☐	☐
3	The witches predict that Macbeth will never be king.	☐	☐
4	The witches tell Banquo that he will be king, but his children will not.	☐	☐
5	The witches vanish.	☐	☐

3 Vocabulary

Listen again to the beginning of Part One. Complete the sentences with a word from the box. You will hear the words in the recording.

> mortal   heath   intrigued   meeting   bravely

1 Macbeth was a brave soldier. He fought .... in every battle.
2 Macbeth and Banquo meet the witches on wild desolate grassland called a ....
3 The witches were hideous and had beards. 'Are you .... ?' asked Banquo.
4 When the third witch called Macbeth 'king', he wanted to know more. He was ....
5 Macbeth and Banquo did not expect to meet witches. It was a strange ....

There was once a thane [1] called Macbeth, who lived in Scotland in the 11th century. He was noble and brave and he was a relative and friend of Duncan, King of Scotland. It was a time when there were many battles. Macbeth had fought bravely against some rebel Scottish nobles and invading Vikings. He was a hero, but as he returned home he did not know that three hideous witches were waiting to meet him. So great were their powers that they had made the sky black and called the fog and wind. Though they were women they had long grey beards and their clothes were long and torn.

'Where's the place?' said the first witch.

'On the heath,' [2] hissed the second.

'Where we'll meet Macbeth,' whispered the third witch.

Macbeth and another Scottish general called Banquo were returning home from the battlefield. As they crossed the heath, thunder rumbled, lightning flashed above them and the three witches appeared. The two generals were afraid when they saw them.

---

1. **thane** : old Scottish word for 'lord'.
2. **heath** : a grassy area of land where there are few trees and bushes.

'Are you mortal?' asked Banquo. 'You look like women, but you have beards.'

'Come on! Tell us who or what you are!' said Macbeth.

The first witch stepped forward. 'Welcome Macbeth, Thane of Glamis.'

Then the second witch said, 'Hail ³ Macbeth, Thane of Cawdor.'

Macbeth was surprised that these strange creatures knew him and even more surprised that they had given him the title "Thane of Cawdor."

Then the third witch called to him, 'Welcome Macbeth, our future king.'

Macbeth was intrigued and he wanted to know more, but the witches had turned their attention to Banquo.

'You are lesser than Macbeth, but greater,' said the first witch.

'You are not so happy, but happier,' said the second witch.

'You will not be king, but your children will sit upon the throne,' said the third witch. Then they vanished into thin air.

'Where have they gone?' said Banquo.

'Into the air,' replied Macbeth.

'Are we going mad?'

'They said that your children will be kings,' said Macbeth.

'They said that you will be king,' replied Banquo.

While they stood talking about their strange meeting, messengers arrived from King Duncan.

'The king has heard of your bravery today in battle, Macbeth,' said Ross, the first messenger. 'He is very pleased and he has given you another title — Thane of Cawdor.'

Macbeth was so surprised he couldn't speak. The witches' words were coming true and he turned to Banquo.

'The witches were right! Don't you hope now that your children will be kings?'

'That hope might lead you to make plans to become king,' answered Banquo. 'Remember that the devil can tempt us to do evil things.'

But the witches' words had sunk deep into Macbeth's mind and he did not listen to Banquo's warning.

'If the witches were right about two things,' Macbeth said to himself,

---

3. **hail** : welcome.

'they can be right about the third, as well.' And from that time, he could only think about how to become King of Scotland.

Macbeth had a wife, a woman who was more ruthless and ambitious than her husband. Macbeth had sent a letter to Lady Macbeth in their castle in Inverness telling her of his meeting with the witches.

'We could be King and Queen of Scotland!' she whispered to herself as she read his letter. 'Why didn't I think of this before?'

Lady Macbeth realised that she would do anything for her husband to become king.

'My husband is ambitious,' she murmured, 'but he is not strong enough.'

When a messenger told her that King Duncan was coming to stay at their castle that evening, Lady Macbeth decided that they would murder him that night.

Macbeth's castle was built in a beautiful place and King Duncan was very pleased when he arrived. He brought his two sons, Malcolm and Donalbain, and a large group of lords and attendants. Lady Macbeth smiled sweetly as she welcomed them, but she wore a mask of deception.

'Look like an innocent flower, but be a serpent underneath,' she said to her husband. She appeared to be the perfect host.

Macbeth was having second thoughts about killing Duncan. Murder was easy, but what about the consequences? Duncan was a good king and Macbeth knew that there was no reason to kill him. But Lady Macbeth was ambitious and she could manipulate her husband. There was nothing that would stop her evil plan. 'If you love me, you will murder Duncan, but if you don't, you are a coward and your love is worth nothing.'

Her plan was this. While Duncan was sleeping, she would give his guards wine to make them drunk. She and Macbeth would slip into Duncan's room and murder him and then smear [4] blood on the sleeping guards. Macbeth agreed. 'I will use every muscle of my body to commit this crime,' he said.

But though Lady Macbeth gave the guards wine to make them sleep, she did not go with Macbeth to murder the king.

4. **smear** : spread.

It was after midnight. Macbeth had just said goodnight to Banquo when a vision of a dagger floated in the air in front of him. The handle of the dagger was pointing towards his hand and the tip towards Duncan's room. When he tried to take the dagger it vanished. It was a dream that came from his troubled mind.

Nearly out of his mind, Macbeth returned to his room, still holding the guards' daggers.

'I have killed him,' he said to Lady Macbeth. 'One of the guards laughed in his sleep and the other cried "murder". I heard a voice say, "You will never sleep again. Macbeth has murdered sleep."'

Macbeth was trembling and his hands and clothes were covered in blood.

'Get some water and wash the blood from your hands,' said Lady Macbeth. 'Why did you bring these daggers here? Take them back to Duncan's room and put some blood on the sleeping guards.'

Macbeth shook his head. 'I can't go back.'

'Coward!' Lady Macbeth said as she took the daggers from him. 'Give them to me. We must make these guards seem guilty.'

And from outside the castle there came the sound of knocking. Taking control of the situation, Lady Macbeth took the daggers back to Duncan's room. Then she ordered Macbeth to wash and change.

The knocking from outside the castle continued and when the porter finally opened the door, Macduff, the Thane of Fife, came in.

'Where's the king?'

'Still asleep,' said Macbeth.

'The king asked me to wake him up early,' said Macduff.

'I'll take you to him,' said Macbeth, but when he let him into the king's bedroom, Macduff came out shouting, 'Help! Help! The king has been murdered!'

'What? In our castle?' said Lady Macbeth. And though Macbeth and his wife pretended to be sad, Macduff was suspicious because Macbeth had killed the guards.

'I killed them in my anger,' Macbeth explained. 'I know it was wrong.'

Duncan's sons were uneasy. Malcolm and Donalbain knew that whoever had killed their father would kill them next. They made their escape. Malcolm went south to England and Donalbain went to Ireland.

When Duncan's sons left, Macbeth was crowned king. The witches' words had come true.

Macbeth and his wife were king and queen, but despite this they could not stop thinking of the witches' prophecy about Banquo and his children. Macbeth often thought that his old friend Banquo was the only man in Scotland he was afraid of. If the witches were right, Macbeth would not have an heir and Banquo's sons would be kings after him. This thought troubled Macbeth so much that he decided that Banquo and his son Fleance had to be killed.

Macbeth organised a great feast. Banquo and Fleance were invited and, after they had ridden to the castle and were dismounting from their horses, three murderers, who had been hired by Macbeth, attacked them. They killed Banquo, but in the dark Fleance escaped. Macbeth was furious when he heard. Fleance was more dangerous than Banquo. He should have been killed and not Banquo.

At the feast, when Macbeth went to take his seat at the head of the royal table, the ghost of Banquo was sitting there. Macbeth's face turned white with fear as he spoke to the ghost. Only Macbeth could see this ghost.

'Get out of here. Get out! I didn't do it!' he shouted at the empty chair.

When the queen and all the thanes saw him speaking to a chair, they thought he had gone mad.

With his mind now tormented with ghosts and visions, Macbeth couldn't sleep any more. He decided to visit the witches again and try to learn more about the future.

The text and **beyond**

1 Comprehension check

Match the beginnings of the sentences (1-6) with the endings (A-F).

1 Three witches predicted that Macbeth
2 The witches also said that
3 Lady Macbeth gave Duncan's guards wine
4 Macbeth stabbed the king
5 Macduff found
6 Macbeth paid assassins to kill Banquo

A ☐ but Fleance, his son, escaped.
B ☐ and then he heard a voice.
C ☐ would be the future king.
D ☐ the murdered king in his bedroom.
E ☐ to make them drunk.
F ☐ Banquo's children would sit upon the throne.

Witches were waiting to meet him.

We use the past continuous to speak about a past activity that has duration and to describe an activity which began before the action expressed by the past simple.
King Duncan was having problems with some of his nobles.
While they were talking about their strange encounter, messengers arrived from the king.

We also use it to describe a scene in the past.
The handle of the dagger was pointing towards his hand.

2 Past simple and past continuous

Complete the sentences. Use the past simple or the past continuous. Choose the verbs from the box.

> sit   want   be (x2)   arrive   shout   see   wait
> knock   have   hold   return   go   read

1 After the battle Macbeth .... a hero, but he did not know that three witches .... for him.
2 Lady Macbeth .... a letter from her husband when a messenger ....
3 Lady Macbeth .... to kill Duncan, but Macbeth .... second thoughts.
4 When Macbeth .... to his room, he .... the daggers.
5 There .... blood on Macbeth's hands and someone .... on the door.
6 Macduff .... when he .... the murdered king's body.
7 When Macbeth .... to the royal table, the ghost of Banquo .... there.

101

3 Synonyms

Find the synonyms of the following words in Part One.

A ugly   ....

B courageous   ....

C callous   ....

D apprehensive   ....

E faint-of-heart ....

F wicked   ....

4 Now use the words to fill in the gaps in the following sentences.

1 Macbeth was a .... thane or lord.
2 The witches with their long grey beards looked ....
3 The witches' words caused Macbeth to think .... thoughts.
4 Lady Macbeth smiled sweetly but she was ....
5 Lady Macbeth could manipulate her husband. She called him a ....
6 Duncan's sons knew that the murderer would kill them. They were ....

Before you read

1 Listening

Listen to the beginning of Part Two. You will hear the part where Macbeth visits the witches. Decide if each sentence is correct or incorrect. If it is correct put a tick (✓) in the box under A for YES. If it is not correct, put a tick (✓) in the box under B for NO.

		A	B
1	The first witch tells her sisters not to call ghosts and spirits when Macbeth comes.	☐	☐
2	A head with a helmet tells Macbeth not to fight with Macduff.	☐	☐
3	Macbeth will be in danger when Birnan Wood moves to Dunsinane Hill.	☐	☐
4	The ghost of Duncan appears covered in blood.	☐	☐
5	The witches answer all of Macbeth's questions.	☐	☐

2 Reading pictures

Look at the pictures on page 105. Answer the questions.

1 Who is in the foreground of the picture?
2 Why is she looking at her hands?
3 Who can you see in the background? What are they doing?

Macbeth rode to a wild and desolate heath. He found the witches in a dark **cave. They were walking around a bubbling** [5] **cauldron** [6] **and into it they threw parts of animals, poisonous plants and the finger of a dead child.**

'Answer the questions I ask you,' said Macbeth.

'You can hear it from us, or the spirits of the dead can answer your questions,' said the first witch.

Macbeth was not afraid. 'Where are they? Let me see them.'

A floating head with a helmet appeared.

'Macbeth, Macbeth, beware of Macduff. Beware of the Thane of Fife.'

'Whatever you are, thank you,' said Macbeth. The head vanished and a child came covered in blood. The child spoke. 'Macbeth, be brave and bold. You cannot be harmed by someone who was born from a woman.'

Next came a child wearing a crown and holding a tree. 'Macbeth, you are safe until Birnan Wood moves to your castle at Dunsinane.'

'Good news,' said Macbeth. 'There is no one who can move a forest. But tell me, will Banquo's children be kings?'

Eight kings walked past Macbeth. The ghost of Banquo followed them, covered in blood. He pointed at the kings and smiled at Macbeth, and Macbeth knew that these were Banquo's children, who would be kings when he was dead.

Macbeth turned to the witches. 'Is this true?' he asked.

5. **bubbling** : containing bubbles rising to the surface.
6. **cauldron** : a large round container for cooking in.

103

'Yes, this is true,' said the first witch. 'Come sisters, let's cheer him up.' The witches danced and then they vanished. Macbeth was left to return home and worry about what he had seen.

The first thing that Macbeth heard when he returned to court was that Macduff had escaped to England to join Malcolm, King Duncan's son. They were raising an army to march against Macbeth and win back the crown of Scotland for Malcolm.

In his fury, Macbeth sent assassins to kill Macduff's wife and children. This terrible act turned all the thanes against him. Everybody hated Macbeth and the murder of Macduff's wife and children was too much for Lady Macbeth. She was by now completely mad. By night she walked in her sleep. She rubbed her hands to try and clean them of the blood of all the men they had murdered.

As a doctor and a lady-in-waiting watched, she began to talk. 'Out, damned spot... I never thought an old man like Duncan could have so much blood in him!... Will these hands never be clean?' She tried to wash them again. Her hands were clean, but to Lady Macbeth they were covered in blood. She tried, but she could not wash her guilt away.

'Can you help her?' the lady-in-waiting asked the doctor, but the doctor shook his head.

'She doesn't need a doctor. She needs a priest,' he said.

And then a cry was heard and the queen, who had been Macbeth's evil companion, killed herself. Macbeth was alone and everyone feared and hated him.

'Life is a story told by an idiot, full of noise and anger — meaning nothing,' Macbeth said in his despair. His queen was dead and suddenly existence didn't have any meaning or purpose. He had grown tired of life and wanted to die. But the arrival of Malcolm's army brought back his courage.

'An English army of ten thousand soldiers is going to attack the castle,' said his messenger, but Macbeth was not afraid. The spirits he had seen in the witches' cave had filled him with hope. He was safe and could not be killed in battle. He was sure that he would die a natural death because the spirits had said that no man born from a woman could kill him. And how could Birnam Wood come to Dunsinane? It was impossible.

'I'm not afraid,' he said, but then the messenger returned.

'The trees of Birnan Wood are advancing towards Dunsinane.'

'The witches' prophecy!' murmured Macbeth. He was terrified, and trembled. Each of Malcolm's soldiers was carrying a branch in front of him to hide the real numbers of the army.

'I cannot run away, but I must fight like a bear,' said Macbeth.

A great battle took place. Malcolm ordered the English soldiers to throw down their tree branches and draw their swords. Macbeth fought with anger and courage and then he finally encountered Macduff, who had been searching for him.

'Beware of Macduff,' the first spirit had said. Macbeth could not run away and Macduff stood in front of him. Remembering the words of the spirit, Macbeth smiled.

'Why should I commit suicide like one of the ancient Romans ?' [3] he said to himself.

'Turn around, you dog from hell,' screamed Macduff.

'You are wasting your time. You cannot harm me, Macduff, because magic surrounds me. I cannot be killed by a man born from a woman.'

'Your magic cannot save you,' laughed Macduff, 'for I was not born from a woman in the usual way. The doctor cut my mother's womb and brought me into this world.'

When he heard this, Macbeth feared for his life. 'I will not fight,' he said.

'Then live!' said Macduff. 'We will lead you in chains through the Scottish villages and towns and show everyone the cruel Macbeth.'

'I don't believe those evil witches any more, but I will not surrender to kiss the ground under young Malcolm's feet. I will make one last attempt,' he said. But though he fought bravely, Macduff was stronger. He killed Macbeth and cut off his head.

'Look, I have Macbeth's head,' Macduff said when he returned to the other soldiers. 'We are free from his tyranny! Join me in this cheer to Malcolm, our true king!'

'Hail Malcolm, King of Scotland,' the soldiers cheered.

'We must call our exiled friends home,' said Malcolm. 'The butcher and his demon queen are dead, and I invite all of you to watch me be crowned King of Scotland.'

---

3. **commit suicide like one of the ancient Romans** : the ancient Romans died in an honourable way by falling on their swords.

The text and **beyond**

FCE **1** **Comprehension check**

For each question, mark the letter next to the correct answer — A, B, C or D.

1   Macbeth wants

  A ☐   a child to answer his questions.

  B ☐   the witches to answer his questions.

  C ☐   the ghost of Duncan to answer his questions.

  D ☐   Macduff to answer his questions.

2   The child spirit tells him he cannot be harmed

  A ☐   by anyone of woman born.

  B ☐   by a woman.

  C ☐   by Macduff.

  D ☐   by the witches.

3   Lady Macbeth keeps washing her hands

  A ☐   because there is blood on them.

  B ☐   because she wants to wash her guilt away.

  C ☐   because her husband is insane.

  D ☐   because the doctor tells her to.

4   Macbeth realises that

  A ☐   Dunsinane Hill is moving towards Birnan Wood.

  B ☐   the army have climbed the trees.

  C ☐   the witches are carrying branches.

  D ☐   each soldier is holding a branch.

5   Macbeth is not afraid to fight Malcolm and his army because

  A ☐   the spirits said he can be killed in battle.

  B ☐   he is a thane.

  C ☐   he is sure that magic surrounds him.

  D ☐   he is stronger than Macduff.

6   Macduff can kill Macbeth because

  A ☐   he was not born of a woman in the usual way.

  B ☐   magic surrounds Macduff.

  C ☐   he is protected by the spirits.

  D ☐   he can fight like a bear.

2 Characters

Answer the questions with the name of one of the characters from the story.

Who...

1   persuaded her husband to kill Duncan?   ....
2   tried to cheer Macbeth up?   ....
3   sleepwalked?   ....
4   killed Macbeth?   ....
5   ordered his soldiers to carry branches?   ....
6   was not interested in the witches' prophecy?   ....
7   gave Macbeth the title of Thane of Cawdor?   ....

3 Famous quotations from the play

Read these quotations from the original version of Shakespeare's *Macbeth*. Match the quotations (1-9) with the characters and what they are saying (A-I).

1   ☐   'Fair is foul and foul is fair.' (Act I, scene i)
2   ☐   'What can the devil speak true?' (Act I, scene iii)
3   ☐   'Yet do I fear thy nature. It is too full o' the milk of human kindness.' (Act I, scene v)
4   ☐   'Come you spirits that tend on mortal thoughts, unsex me here. And fill me from the crown to the toe top-full of direst cruelty!' (Act I, scene v)
5   ☐   'Is this a dagger which I see before me, the handle toward my hand?' (Act II, scene i)
6   ☐   'Methought I heard a voice cry "Sleep no more!" Macbeth does murder sleep.' (Act II, scene ii)
7   ☐   'Out damned spot! Out I say!' (Act V, scene i)
8   ☐   'Life's but a walking shadow, a poor player that struts and frets his hour upon the stage and then is heard no more: it is a tale told by an idiot full of sound and fury signifying nothing.' (Act V, scene v)
9   ☐   'Macduff was from his mother's womb untimely ripp'd.' (Act V, scene viii)

A   After receiving her husband's letter about the witches prophecy, Lady Macbeth expresses her fear that he isn't bad enough.
B   Lady Macbeth's sleepwalking scene.
C   The witches' philosophy on life.
D   Banquo's reaction when he finds that Macbeth has been named Thane of Cawdor, as the witches predicted.
E   Macbeth despairs when he hears about his wife's death.
F   Macbeth sees the vision of a bloody dagger leading the way.
G   Macduff tells Macbeth that he is not born of a woman.
H   After murdering King Duncan, Macbeth fears he will not sleep any more.
I   Lady Macbeth when she knows that she must find the courage to murder King Duncan when he stays at their castle.

T: GRADE **8**

4 **Speaking – Public figures past and present**

Macbeth was a real 11th century Scottish king. In 1040 he killed King Duncan I in a battle near Elgin. Talk to a partner about a famous public figure from the past. Ask and answer the questions.

1   Who is this famous person and when did they live?
2   Why are they famous?
3   What did they achieve in their lives?
4   Why do you like or admire them?
5   Is it necessary to become ruthless to get to the top?

5 **Writing**

You recently went to a murder mystery weekend in Scotland. You enjoyed it, but you are writing to make some suggestions as to how to improve these weekends. Read the advertisement and the notes you made beside it. Then write a letter to the organisers.

Lady Macbeth's Murder Mystery Weekends
at
Dunsinane Castle
Every weekend in August

Deluxe 5 star accommodation
Wonderful à la carte dining
Relax in our pool and spa

Be entertained by our talented actors
and join in as you try to work out
who killed King Duncan!
Come... you'll have a murderous time!

Why not all year round?

My room was small and cold.

The food was awful!

The actors were wonderful... really scary.

Lovely mountain walks.

The pool was too cold.

Write your letter in 120-180 words in an appropriate style. Do not write any addresses. Before you write answer these questions.

1   Who are you writing to?
2   Why are you writing the letter?
3   How many suggestions do you want to make in your letter?
4   Will you write *Yours sincerely* or *Yours faithfully* at the end of the letter?

1 **Picture summary**

Look at the pictures from the book *Power and Ambition in Shakespeare*. Decide which pictures belong to which story. There are three for each story. Put them in the order in which they occur in the stories.

		1	2	3
1	*Richard III*	☐	☐	☐
2	*Henry V*	☐	☐	☐
3	*Julius Caesar*	☐	☐	☐
4	*Hamlet*	☐	☐	☐
5	*Macbeth*	☐	☐	☐

A ☐   B ☐   C ☐

D ☐   E ☐   F ☐

G ☐   H ☐   I ☐

2 Pictures into words

What might the characters be saying or thinking in each picture? Invent phrases
or sentences to put in speech and/or thought balloons, and write captions under
the pictures to narrate what is happening.

3 A poster

Make a poster to advertise one of the stories. Use copies of pictures from this
book, short extracts from the story, words and pictures of your own and from
other sources.

This reader uses the **EXPANSIVE READING** approach, where the text becomes a springboard to improve language skills and to explore historical background, cultural connections and other topics suggested by the text.

The new structures introduced in this step of our **R**EADING & **T**RAINING series are listed below. Naturally, structures from lower steps are included too. For a complete list of structures used over all the six steps, see *The Black Cat Guide to Graded Readers*, which is also downloadable at no cost from our website, blackcat-cideb.com.

The vocabulary used at each step is carefully checked against vocabulary lists used for internationally recognised examinations.

Step **Four B2.1**

All the structures used in the previous levels, plus the following:

Verb tenses

Present Perfect Simple: *the first / second* etc. *time that ...*

Present Perfect Continuous: unfinished past with *for* or *since* (duration form)

Verb forms and patterns

Passive forms: Present Perfect Simple

Reported speech introduced by precise reporting verbs (e.g. *suggest, promise, apologise*)

Modal verbs

Be / get used to + *-ing*: habit formation

Had better: duty and warning

Types of clause

3rd Conditional: *if* + Past Perfect, *would(n't) have*

Conditionals with *may / might*

Non-defining relative clauses with: *which, whose*

Clauses of concession: *even though*; *in spite of, despite*